ANCIENT PERUVIAN CERAMICS

ANCIENT PERUVIAN CERAMICS

THE NATHAN CUMMINGS COLLECTION

by Alan R. Sawyer WITH DRAWINGS

BY MILTON F. SONDAY, JR. AND PHOTOGRAPHS BY

WILLIAM F. PONS AND WILLIAM E. LYALL

THE METROPOLITAN MUSEUM OF ART

DISTRIBUTED BY New York Graphic Society, GREENWICH, CONNECTICUT

THIS IS NUMBER *373*

OF AN EDITION OF 500 COPIES

Alan R. Sawyer

Designed by Peter Oldenburg. Composed in Palatino by
Finn Typographic Service, Inc. Printed in an edition of
12,500 copies on Stevens-Nelson Text by The Meriden
Gravure Company. Color plates made and printed by
Conzett & Huber, Zurich, Switzerland. Bound by Russell-
Rutter Company.

PREFACE

The trained eye and connoisseurship of Alan R. Sawyer, his practical field experience in Peruvian archaeology are well known. His intimate association in helping Mr. Cummings in the building of his collection of Peruvian pottery since its inception, and his appreciation of its great historical and artistic interest suggested that Mr. Sawyer rather than anyone else should prepare this fascinating factual treatise. We are grateful to Mr. Sawyer and to the Trustees of The Textile Museum in Washington, of which he is the Director, for granting the time required to prepare this book.

The generosity of Mr. and Mrs. Nathan Cummings in presenting the major part of the collection described in the following pages and their making possible this publication is indeed appreciated by the Trustees and the staff of The Metropolitan Museum of Art.

JAMES J. RORIMER
Director

CONTENTS

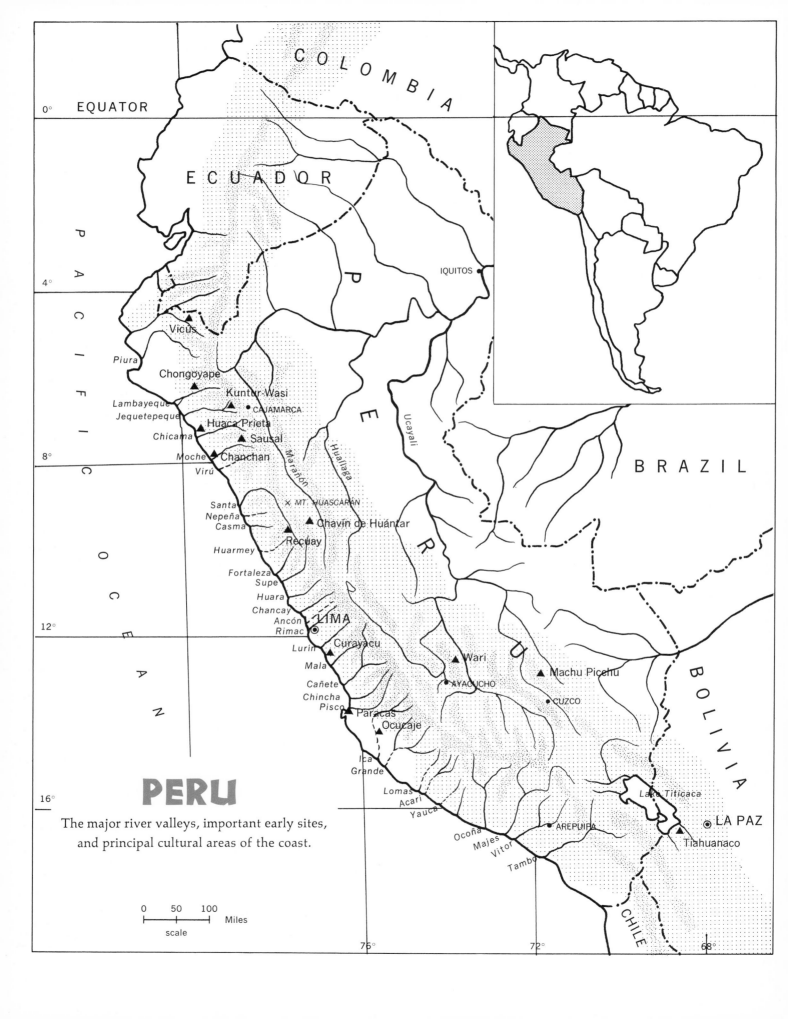

COLOMBIA

EQUATOR 0°

ECUADOR

P

IQUITOS

4°

PACIFIC

Vicus

Piura

Chongoyape

Kuntur-Wasi

Lambayeque
Jequetepeque · CAJAMARCA

Huaca Prieta

Chicama

Sausal

8° Moche Chanchan

Virú

Marañón

Huallaga

Ucayali

BRAZIL

Santa
Nepeña
Casma

× MT. HUASCARÁN

Chavín de Huántar

Recuay

Huarmey

E

Fortaleza
Supe
Huara
Chancay
Ancón LIMA
Rimac

12° Lurín Curayacu

Mala

Cañete
Chincha
Pisco Paracas

Ocucaje

R

Wari

Machu Picchu

AYACUCHO

CUZCO

U

BOLIVIA

Ica
Grande

16° Lomas
Acari
Yauca

Ocoña
Majes
Vitor

Tambo

Lake Titicaca

AREQUIPA

LA PAZ

Tiahuanaco

PERU

The major river valleys, important early sites,
and principal cultural areas of the coast.

CHILE

0   50   100
|——|——| Miles
scale

75°   72°   68°

1 INTRODUCTION

PERU OCCUPIES the central portion of the mighty Andean mountain chain that closely parallels the western edge of South America. Here the blue Pacific pounds a narrow ribbon of surf against a 1,300-mile-long coast of jagged rocks and empty beaches. The narrow coastal plain is an ashen desert crowded by parched mountain spurs, which rise in awesome crescendo to lofty snow-capped peaks. The highest, Mt. Huascarán, over 22,200 feet in altitude and only sixty miles from the sea, forms part of the continental watershed. Cool winds from offshore are heated by the sun-scorched desert and, taking rather than giving moisture, rise upward as they move inland, until at last the altitude wrings them dry. Most of the precipitation flows rapidly into tributaries of the Amazon, which reach like tentacles into the heart of the mountains, drawing off moisture to be lavished on steaming jungle and swamp. Only a fraction of the water drains toward the Pacific, through about forty steep-walled valleys, many of which are dry much of the year. The fact that this arid mountain-crowded zone between jungle and sea gave rise to some of the most splendid of ancient American civilizations is a tribute to man's extraordinary ability to cooperate with his kind to overcome the most hostile of environments.

When the first human inhabitants roamed the central Andean area, about 11,000 years ago, the climate was not as harsh as it is today. Ample rain supported forests and grasslands in the highland and coastal valleys. Small nomadic bands of Stone Age men could easily subsist by hunting, fishing, and the gathering of wild fruits and vegetables. For several thousand years there was a gradual change in this way of life as the area became more and more arid, and the population was forced to concentrate in the few well-watered areas. We know almost nothing of the history of the highlands during this period, but on the coast vast shell heaps mark the location of early settlements, situated to reap the abundant harvest of the seashore. By 4000 B.C. some of these villages were practicing limited agriculture, raising such vegetables as beans, squash, and chili peppers to supplement wild food supplies.

Inhabitants of the first agricultural communities fashioned tools, weapons, and ornaments from stone, bone, shell, and wood. They had no ceramics, but made containers for food and liquids from bottle gourds, which they raised for that

1

2

purpose. Baskets and mats were woven from rushes; other vegetable fibers, which by 3000 B.C. included domesticated cotton, provided material for nets and textiles.

The earliest known art objects from ancient Peru were found in one of these early, pre-ceramic village sites. In stratified refuse at Huaca Prieta, on the north coast near the mouth of the Chicama River, Junius B. Bird discovered fragments of decorated cotton textiles dating from 2500 to 2000 B.C. By carefully charting the warp movements in the twined fabrics, Dr. Bird has been able to reconstruct a large variety of highly stylized motifs, including condors (1), human figures, serpents, crabs, and pumas. He also found the fragile remains of two small gourds, their surfaces ornamented in low relief by cutting away the background and incising the inner details of the motifs. One is embellished with four boldly simplified frontal heads (2), possibly feline, while the other bears two similar faces attached to abstract and evidently anthropomorphic bodies, alternating with bird-headed serpents. The lid of the second exhibits an S-shaped device ending in bird heads, a motif also found on Huaca Prieta textiles. Dr. Bird's important discoveries, made possible by his skillful application of the most advanced scientific procedures, shine a thin ray of light into that remote and little-understood era in which Peru's civilizations began. The art of this humble village is surprisingly sophisticated and perhaps reflects developments at some more important but as

3

4

yet unknown center. In both motifs and design conventions it forecasts much of the religious iconography of the great periods of ancient Peruvian culture that followed.

From 1500 to 1000 B.C., a number of important new technological advances appeared in Peru. They included domesticated maize, techniques of building with preformed adobes, the working of stone and metals, and the making of pottery. These innovations were manifestations of a startling acceleration of cultural progress throughout most of the central Andean region. In the matter of a few centuries, the northern people were united by a vigorous religious cult, called Chavín after its best-known highland ceremonial center, Chavín de Huántar. Here massive temples were built of finely dressed stone and embellished with spectacular friezes in low relief, carved columns, and other sculptural ornament. The subjects depicted were awesome feline-fanged deities (4), and dynamic birds of prey (3) and felines (5). Simplified versions of these powerful motifs and symbols derived from them were used by the Chavín craftsmen to ornament their well-made ceramics, beautiful objects of gold, silver, stone, shell, and bone, and textiles woven in a variety of techniques. Progress in the arts was matched by the growth of political and social institutions, and an increase in agricultural productivity achieved by improved irrigation and terracing.

5

The widespread influence of Chavín religion and the advanced technology associated with it acted as catalysts for the development of several distinctive regional cultures. Outstanding among these are the Mochica, which flourished on the north coast, and the Paracas on the south coast that, from similar Chavinoid beginnings, passed through a series of evolutionary stages to become the Nazca culture. In many ways, the craft achievements of these two peoples represent the apogee of ancient Peruvian art. For this reason, the period they represent has been called the Master-Craftsman, Florescent, or Classic period. Outstanding examples of ceramic art in the Nathan Cummings Collection offer us an unusual opportunity to document the history and character of both the Mochica and the Paracas civilizations. The collection also contains sufficient examples of subsequent styles for us to trace the major trends in pottery down to the time of the Spanish conquest.

The upper Ica Valley, as it wends its way into the mountains several miles to the northeast of Teojate

The purpose of this handbook is to aid the interested layman and student in the understanding and appreciation of an outstanding collection of ancient Peruvian ceramics. The treatment of the two major groups will, of necessity, be quite different. Mochica ceramics have already been studied and published in detail. Their stylistic development was simple and logical and their subject matter realistically presented, making interpretation relatively easy. The evolution of the Paracas culture was, on the other hand, extremely complex, and has not yet been adequately clarified by archaeological fieldwork. Its confusing array of styles is characterized by abstract religious symbols that lack the story-telling qualities of Mochica iconography. I shall attempt in both cases to present my own interpretation of available archaeological data, without such scholarly appurtenances as polemics and footnotes. A selected bibliography is included for the reader who would like to explore the fascinating realm of ancient Peruvian art in more detail.

RELATIVE CHRONOLOGY OF
THE NORTH AND SOUTH COASTS OF PERU

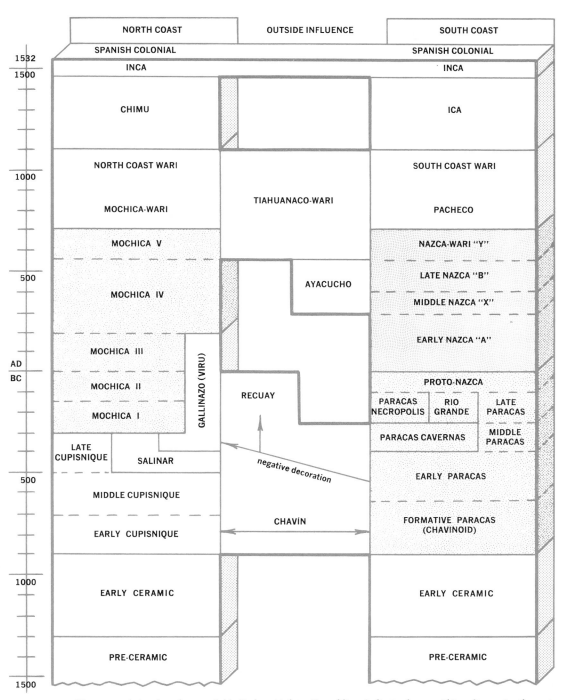

NOTE: Dates are relative, based on available Carbon 14 data. Dotted lines indicate phases within cultures. South coast
chronology applicable specifically to the Ica Valley.

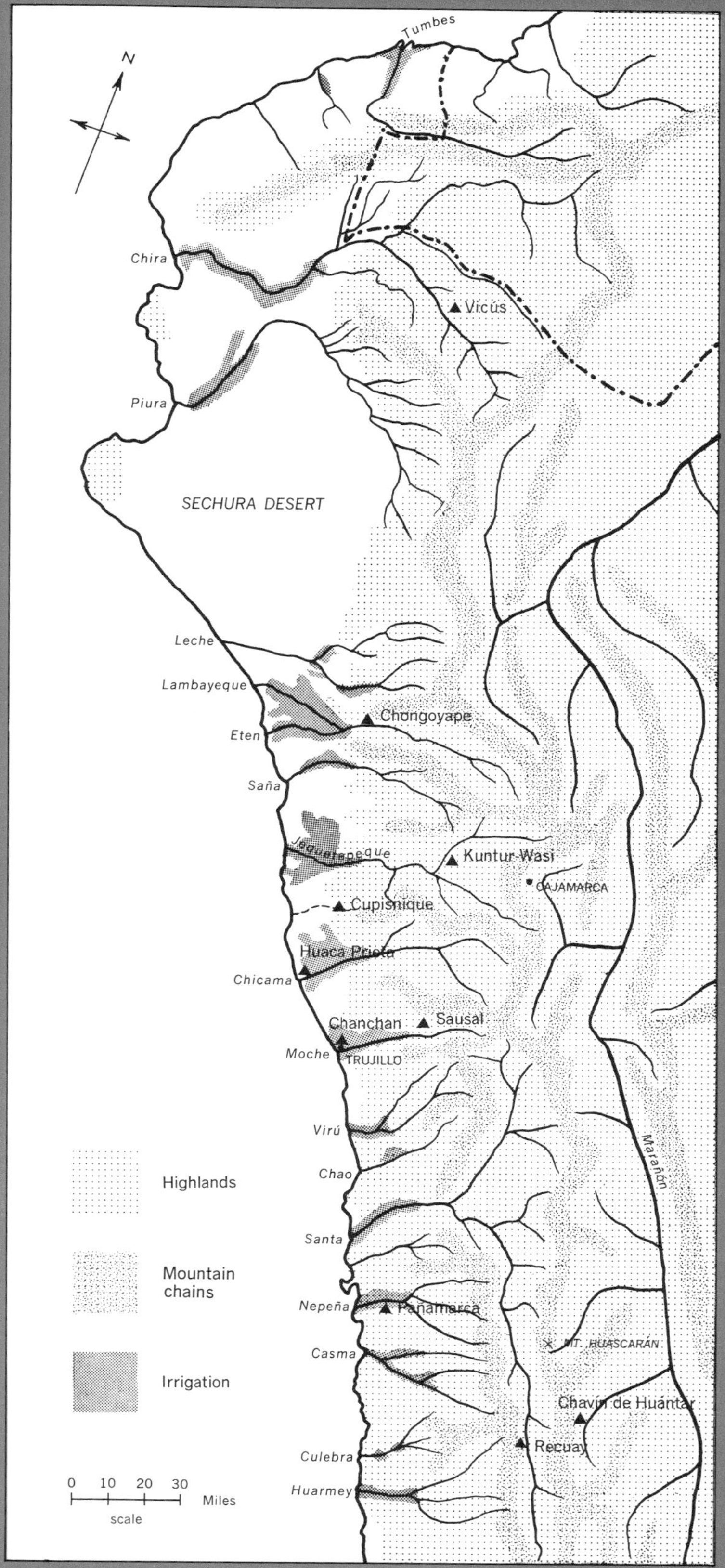

THE NORTH COAST

Tumbes

Chira

Vícus

Piura

SECHURA DESERT

Leche

Lambayeque

Eten ▲ Chongoyape

Saña

Jequetepeque ▲ Kuntur Wasi

• CAJAMARCA

▲ Cupisnique

Huaca Prieta

Chicama ▲

Chanchan ▲ Sausal

Moche ▲ TRUJILLO

Virú

Chao

Santa

Nepeña ▲ Pañamarca

Casma

× MT. HUASCARÁN

Chavín de Huántar

▲ Recuay

Culebra

Huarmey

Marañón

Highlands

Mountain chains

Irrigation

0 10 20 30 Miles
scale

2 THE FORMATIVE PERIOD

6

THE MOCHICA, one of the most vigorous and prosperous cultures of ancient Peru, first appeared in the Chicama and Moche river valleys in the fourth century B.C. It emerged from a period of intense interaction between the local Chavinoid culture, called Cupisnique, and two intrusive groups, named Salinar and Gallinazo. Just as a new and hardier plant strain is produced by cross-pollination with other varieties, the Mochica drew important elements from each of its predecessors to form its own distinctive character. We know very little about the origin and history of these earlier cultures, but a brief examination of their ceramics will serve to demonstrate the contribution each made to the emerging Mochica style.

CUPISNIQUE

Early Cupisnique ceramics closely resembled those of highland Chavín. They were well made and polished, though somewhat thick-walled and heavy. The type of firing used produced a dark semireduced ware that varied from brownish gray to carbon black in color. Decoration consisted of bold, curvilinear human, feline, and bird of prey heads, eye patterns, pelt markings, and other brief symbols of the central motifs featured in the large Chavín stone reliefs, together with simple geometric devices. All were executed in broad incised lines and were often set off by textural treatment of the background. This technique was a natural outgrowth of the pre-ceramic tradition of carving and pyroengraving gourds. The forms of decorative Cupisnique ceramics were few, consisting mostly of simple bowls and two distinctive bottle shapes, of which one was a flasklike vessel closely resembling the form of the bottle gourd (6). The other had a spherical body with a flattened base, and was surmounted by a hollow archlike handle with a spout projecting from its center (7). Although this "stirrup-spout" bottle is known to have occurred in Chavín ceramics and in an even earlier style in Ecuador, its origins are obscure. It was later adopted by both the Salinar and Gallinazo cultures, became the most typical Mochica ceramic type, and continued to be characteristic of the north coast down to the time of the Spanish conquest.

During the Middle Cupisnique period, three distinct types of ceramic ornamentation began to emerge, which were to become the basic modes of the later

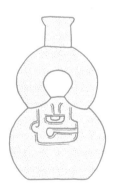

7

8

Mochica style. The first type refined incised lines and textural effects as a means of surface decoration (7, 8, the latter a Late Cupisnique example). The second, evidently suggested by the repoussé effect of broad-line incising, became relief, and the third, an outgrowth of relief, developed toward fully modeled three-dimensional forms. The subject matter, in this Middle period, remained strongly Chavinoid.

Late Cupisnique ceramics manifest the strong influence exerted on the culture by intrusive groups that we will presently discuss. Pottery became much more varied in technique, and subject matter broadened to include a wide range of non-Chavinoid elements. Sculptural vessels gained importance, with human (9), animal, bird, vegetable, marine, and architectural forms forecasting Mochica themes.

9

SALINAR

Sometime around the fifth century B.C., the Salinar culture moved into the north coast of Peru, spread its influence throughout the Cupisnique area, and soon dominated parts of the Chicama and nearby valleys. Salinar pottery, though deceptively primitive in ornamentation, was technologically superior to that of the Cupisnique. Vessels were made of well-prepared clays that were fully oxidized in firing, making them an even orange in color. Cream and red slips were used to accentuate sculptural forms and to create flat geometric patterns, but not to draw figurative motifs. The technical advances of controlled oxidation firing and slip decoration soon had their effect on contemporary Cupisnique ceramics, which gradually became predominantly polychrome (11).

The Salinar culture introduced two new bottle types that we should mention here, since we will have occasion to refer to them later. One had a central spout with a strap handle leading from it to the shoulder of the vessel (10). Variations of this form are found occasionally among later Mochica ceramics. The second bottle form had a straight, open spout at one side of the top surface, with a bridge-like handle leading to a modeled blind spout on the other (12). This distinctive

10

ceramic type may have originated on the south coast, where it appears in the earliest Formative Paracas period levels (13) and passes through a long evolution until it finally becomes the familiar Nazca double-spout and bridge bottle. Its appearance in Salinar suggests a northward diffusion of traits following the southward spread of Chavinoid influence. Whatever the explanation of this enigma may prove to be, both single- and double-spout bottles with strap handles continued to be characteristic of the area north of the Mochica heartland and reappeared throughout the north coast in the later, Chimú period.

13

GALLINAZO

While the Salinar and Cupisnique cultures were interacting in the Chicama and Moche valleys, they were supplanted in the Virú (the next valley to the south) by a new intrusive group called Gallinazo. The Gallinazo, together with the closely related Recuay culture that now appeared in the nearby highlands, formed part of the so-called negative horizon that seems to have resulted from a second wave of influence from the south coast. All cultures of this horizon shared such early south coast traits as negative decoration and whistle-spout vessels, such as the Gallinazo example shown in Figure 14.

14

Negative decoration was achieved by painting designs onto the fired ceramic with clay. The vessel was then coated with a material that charred when exposed to fire, causing a carbon impregnation of the surface not protected by the clay resist. Whistle spouts were usually modeled in the form of a head or figure; they contained a hollow sphere with a hole in one side and vents so arranged that a jet of air passed over the hole, causing it to whistle whenever the liquid in the container was sloshed or air was forced through the other, open spout. The original significance may have been to give a voice to an inanimate object used in ritual, although later usage may have had a less serious intent. The negative technique of decoration was not adopted in the emerging Mochica style, although a fugitive black, added after firing, was evidently accomplished in a similar manner (15; the drawing is taken from the stirrup-spout vessel illustrated as Figure 25 on page 27). The peculiar whistle-spout vessel did continue as a minor Mochica ceramic type (16).

The Gallinazo culture remained in control of the Virú Valley throughout the early formative periods of Mochica, but was overwhelmed when that culture expanded, around the turn of the Christian era, to incorporate other valleys.

15

16

RECUAY

Very little is known about the history and development of the Recuay culture, which evidently had established itself in the vast intermountain valley called the Callejón de Huaylas soon after 500 B.C. Its ceramics were decorated with negative designs closely coordinated with bands of cream and red slip and highly stylized modeled elements (17). Unlike the more primitive Gallinazo wares, which bore dot, line, and other simple geometric negative patterns, the Recuay used panels containing figure motifs — animals, birds, and serpents.

Recuay-related ceramics are sometimes found on the coast in Gallinazo context and are encountered in upper reaches of valleys such as the Santa, and their influence on the formative stages of the Mochica style was surprisingly strong. Typical Recuay motifs, such as highly stylized plumed pumas and triangular-headed serpents, are often found on early Mochica ceramics (18), though rendered in slip rather than in the negative technique. The strength of this influence suggests that the early Mochica people may have included groups that had been in close contact with the Recuay culture during the interval in which they had been forced out of their homeland by the Salinar and Gallinazo occupations. We will need much more information concerning the archaeology of the north coast and highlands of Peru before this and many other questions dealing with the formation of the Mochica culture can be answered with certainty. For the present, we can only observe that the Recuay culture appears to have reinforced the tradition of figure motifs drawn in line in the development of the Mochica slip-painted style.

17

VICÚS

When I wrote the first Nathan Cummings Collection handbook twelve years ago, there were still many archaeologists who interpreted the Cupisnique-Salinar-Gallinazo-Mochica sequence as the continuous evolution of a single culture. Present evidence favors the view then held by Dr. Bird and others that the Mochica civilization developed directly out of the Cupisnique, though subject to Salinar, Gallinazo, and Recuay influence. In recent years, a large quantity of pottery and other artifacts said to have come from Vicús, a site in the north Peruvian highlands close to the Ecuadorian border, have appeared on the antiquities market. They promise to furnish interesting new evidence bearing on this problem.

Vicús ceramics are said to come from clandestine excavations of prehistoric cemeteries on the Hacienda Pabur, near the town of Ayabaca. No archaeologist has yet conducted field research in the area, but the pottery styles themselves suggest an unbroken transition from Chavinoid pottery similar to Cupisnique to ceramics closely resembling early Mochica types found 250 miles to the south.

19

20

Most of the latter are modeled wares such as the owl shown here (20). I have also seen slip-decorated vessels with motifs sometimes outlined by incised lines, and others with low-relief geometric designs set off by textural treatment of the surface in a manner reminiscent of the Chavinoid style.

This Chavinoid, early Mochica style appears to have been supplanted at Vicús by ceramics combining Salinar and Gallinazo traits, such as negative decoration, the use of cream and red slips, and modeling that is very primitive compared to earlier naturalism. An engaging family group of double-chambered vessels (19), with whistles in their heads, illustrates the later type. This sequence of styles reinforces the theory that ceramics with Salinar and Gallinazo characteristics are independent of the Chavinoid-Mochica development, and are outside infusions rather than stages in its evolution.

21

3 MOCHICA CHRONOLOGY

THE MOCHICA civilization appears to have flourished for nearly one thousand years, during which time it passed through a succession of evolutionary stages that Rafael Larco Hoyle, Peru's foremost authority on north coast cultures, has divided into five chronological periods. The first two are formative phases, wherein a great deal of experimentation took place, and each urban center tended to reflect the peculiar combination of influences to which it had been subjected. The Mochica culture and its distinctive art style crystallized in the third period, flourished throughout the fourth, and gradually declined in the fifth. A few examples will serve to illustrate this stylistic evolution.

MOCHICA I

Mochica I modeled ceramics show a strong continuation of the Late Cupisnique sculptural style. The forms are compact (22), with little suggestion of action, and details are often rendered in incised lines. Faces are generalized, but individual personages are differentiated by costume and accessories, and by distinctive physical traits.

Painted pottery of this period is relatively rare. When it occurs, it usually bears geometric designs like those of Salinar, although, as in our illustration (21), Recuay-derived figure motifs appear occasionally. The use of colored slips differs from Salinar precedents in that the vessel was first entirely covered with cream slip and then the decorative motifs were painted over it in red. Sometimes, as in Late Cupisnique pottery, incised lines were used to outline painted designs.

23

24

MOCHICA II

By Period II the techniques of slip decoration and oxidation firing were well mastered, though some semireduced wares (gray to brown) were still being made. Painted ornament continued to be predominantly geometric (26), and figure motifs, when attempted, were rendered in silhouette. Low relief (24) was often used in preference to painted decoration, especially to depict mythological scenes or other subjects requiring a suggestion of action. Relief-decorated ceramics incorporated two concave sections made in the same mold, usually joined by a broad band of clay into which the stirrup spout was inserted. Our late Period II example with ducks in relief (25) is an exception to this rule, in that no intermediate band is apparent and the halves were evidently joined directly together.

Relief-decorated wares appear to have been the first type of Mochica ceramic to be made in a mold. The mold technique was now applied to all sculptural vessels, and, due to the necessity of avoiding undercuts, became an important factor in increasing their frontality and simplicity of form. Vessels in the shape of a head or of a figure (23) required two or more molds, one usually forming the front and the other the back. Projecting details such as arms or headdress ornaments, as well as stirrup spouts, were added after the basic form had been assembled. Many vessels made from the same molds exist in which the only differences are the result of finishing.

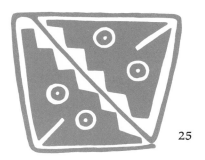

25

27

MOCHICA III

In the third period, the Mochica ceramic style developed steadily in the direction of realism. Modeling became increasingly naturalistic (27) and painting gradually more animated, shifting from silhouette to line, with greater attention to costume detail. Highly polished and lustrous black reduction wares, in relief or fully modeled (27, 29), enjoyed great popularity, along with beautifully oxidized orange ware vessels remarkable for the opacity of their cream and red slip decoration (28). At times a third color, orange, was used, as was the fugitive black adapted from the Gallinazo negative technique. The fresh vigor of the newly matured style produced some of the Mochica's finest ceramics. Social, political, and religious institutions enjoyed a corresponding unification and maturity, which enabled the Mochica to move outward from the Chicama and Moche valleys and dominate neighboring groups by either military or religious conquest.

28

29

30

31

MOCHICA IV

The fourth period, the golden age of the Mochica, saw an extensive kingdom established and consolidated. It brought together the inhabitants of all north coast valleys, from the Lambayeque to the Casma, in a closely unified culture that allowed little regional variation of style. The painted pieces were decorated in flowing, expressive line (30), while modeled pottery showed great attention to individual character and costume (32).

Toward the end of this long period, ceramics began to become mannered and sometimes evidence a decline in Mochica vitality (31), which may have resulted from an overrigid control enforced by the ruling warrior-priest class. Both the subject matter and the style of ceramic art had become so strictly prescribed that little latitude was left for the craftsman's creative imagination.

32

33

34

MOCHICA V

In the fifth and last Mochica period, ceramic art, although still displaying an occasional flare of brilliance, settled into a stage of decadence. Modeled wares (33) lost the careful attention to sculptural detail and finish that had characterized them earlier, and painted designs tended to be overcrowded and, all too often, carelessly done. Purely geometric designs enjoyed a renewed popularity (34). The period

35

was one in which the Mochica culture was being subjected to increasing pressure from a militant, expansionist group, the highland Tiahuanaco culture called Wari. Ceramics seem to reflect a nervousness and tension that sometimes were expressed with bristling energy or, more often, yielded to apathy — a contrast shown in Figures 35 and 36, two versions of a common Period V motif, a hawk eating from a bowl. The struggle between the Mochica and Wari was long and fierce, ending with the complete collapse of Mochica culture and the abrupt termination of the great art tradition that had expressed it so well.

35

36

37

OPPOSITE: *Ruins of Pañamarca, a Mochica IV ceremonial center in the Nepeña Valley. The adobe walls and the ziggurat-like temple pyramid at the left were originally covered with colorful murals*

4 MOCHICA CERAMIC ART

THE MOCHICA ceramic style is essentially realistic, and covers a broad range of subject matter encompassing many aspects of Mochica life. For this reason, the pottery reveals far more about the civilization that produced it than does that of any other Peruvian culture. Most art styles limited their ceramic decoration to a rather small vocabulary of abstract religious symbols. Mochica ceramics also dealt with religious subject matter, but that religion expressed itself in ceremony and mythology in which the individual and all nature played a vital role.

The realism of Mochica ceramics can be misleading. It is as if we were in possession of the illustrations of ancient books, the texts of which are lost. We must be mindful, as we attempt to place the pictures in order and reconstruct their story, that we are incapable of deciphering their full meaning. We may watch a colorful ceremony or the unfolding of a myth, but never fully comprehend its significance. We will see men playing flutes, but their melody has long since been carried away on the winds of time.

PORTRAITURE

The most unusual and perhaps best-known type of Mochica ceramic is the portrait-head vessel (37). Early Mochica portrait heads tended to be generalized, and individuals were identified by face painting or some other distinctive feature (38). Portraiture reached its full development late in Period III and played a significant role in Mochica art throughout the great period of realism that followed. The heads usually took the form of a stirrup-spout bottle or a jar open at the top,

38

39, 40

and averaged slightly more than half life size (39, 40). Their remarkable individuality suggests that the original model may have been made from life, probably in clay that was not fired. (No such model has survived, although fired sectional molds taken from them are found.)

As one becomes familiar with Mochica portraits, he begins to recognize individual personages as he encounters them in publications and museums throughout the world. In the more extensive archaeological collections of Peru, one often finds groups of portraits of the same individual. Some of these are obviously

39, 40

OPPOSITE: 41, 42, 43

44, 45, 46

duplicates made from the same mold, while others may represent the man at different stages of his life, or portray members of the same family group. It appears obvious that the portraits were of rulers or other powerful leaders, and that the presence of a portrait-head vessel in a grave signified an honor bestowed upon the deceased.

The importance of the portrait to the Mochica is attested to by the care with which the vessels were polished and reworked with stone and bone tools after the molded sections had been assembled. The likeness was rendered skillfully with sculptural simplicity, but with a full understanding of the subtle complexity of facial planes. Details of the headdress, ear ornaments, and face-painting designs, all evidently significant in establishing the rank and identity of the subject, were kept subordinate to the plastic three-dimensionality of the face.

47, 48, 49

FIGURE VESSELS

Modeled figure vessels portray a much larger group of subjects than the head vessels, although some of the same individuals are included. We see dignified leaders, religious functionaries and mystics (50), stalwart warriors, and humble servants. Merchants and craftsmen (52) are shown displaying their wares, and women carry burdens (51) or tend their children. The heads of these figures were made disproportionately large, and many show the same careful attention to individual likeness that characterizes the portrait vessels. Together, the two categories of ceramics show the Mochica to be a mixed race, with physical types covering a wide range. There are some that conform to our contemporary image of American Indians, but many could easily be mistaken for Europeans, Asians, or Africans (41-49).

50

51

52

53

Individuals suffering from physical deformity or the ravages of disease were frequent subjects of the Mochica potters (54-56). Their unnatural appearance may have been attributed to their being possessed by supernatural spirits, which were thought to give them extraordinary powers. For this reason, hunchbacks, dwarfs, lepers, and blind men perhaps performed religious functions such as those of shaman or seer. Today these representations are of unique importance to medical historians.

The modeled figures (53), together with those rendered in line on painted pottery, provide us with extensive documentation on costume, which varied considerably, depending on the period and the individual's rank and function in Mochica society. Few of the actual fabrics and accessories survive, due to the unfavorable conditions for preservation of organic materials on the north coast. We must therefore lean heavily on ceramic evidence to interpret the few fragments of costume that remain.

54, 55, 56

57

WARRIORS

58

The warrior class played a vital role in the ceremonial life of the Mochica people, as well as in the defense of their territory. Their status seems to have been similar to that of the medieval knights of Europe, and their apparel, which was elaborate for pageantry and functional for combat, bore the distinctive heraldic devices of their order and rank (57). An ornamental but simple tunic, belted at the waist and sometimes with short sleeves, was the main item of dress. It was often harlequin in design, and metal disks and plates added glitter as well as armored protection. Since clubs were the chief fighting weapons and the head the main target, helmets were sturdily designed. The most common type was a casque, evidently made of wood, leather, and copper, which had an armored neck-piece and a chin strap, to which ornamental ear protectors were attached. Another was a well-padded turban, sometimes covered with an ocelot or bird skin. Both types were embellished with metal crestings and feather ornaments.

In addition to the tunic and helmet, the warriors generally wore wide, protective collars and cuffs, and a peculiar device attached to the belt at the back. In modeled versions, the latter can be seen to be an armored tailpiece made of copper, wood, and leather; two gilded copper fittings in the Cummings collection (58) appear to be clasps from these, with loops for thongs to attach them to the belt. The faces, arms, and legs of the warriors were painted, in the last case making it appear as if long stockings with knee patches were worn.

In modeled versions warriors are usually depicted on one knee, holding their clubs and shields to the front (60), a posture that was evidently the Mochica equivalent of "present arms." At other times they are shown sleeping, fully dressed in a seated position (59), as if on call for duty. On painted vessels we see

59, 60

63

62

them in more active poses, while engaged in ceremonial processions and scenes of combat. Generally all combatants are shown in Mochica costume, although sometimes warriors with different weapons and dress are represented. The former suggest reenactments of historic events or perhaps ceremonial jousting, while in the latter the enemy is inevitably getting the worst of it, and we are undoubtedly being given the Mochica version of an actual battle. Although throwing sticks, darts, and slings were used, probably when closing with the enemy, the Mochica's most formidable weapon was his heavy-headed club with a long copper spike attached to the handle. He used this weapon much as the modern soldier uses bayonet and gun butt. Defeated warriors were taken prisoner, stripped of their costumes and weapons, bound, and led away in disgrace. The arms and armor, symbolizing the rank and prowess of the vanquished, became the trophies of the victor.

The two principal orders or classes of Mochica warriors were associated with the fox and the hawk. The fox was one of the largest land animals of the north coast area, and it is likely that then as now he was known for his cunning as well as his fleetness. His white underbody and dark top were evidently the inspiration for the harlequin costume characteristic of the order. In some representations (61-63) it is difficult to say whether a warrior wearing a fox mask and tail is depicted, or whether the representation is symbolically anthropomorphic.

64

Other warriors are shown in painted versions with the face, wings, tail, and sometimes the raptorial feet of the hawk, as in our elaborate Period V example (64). This ornately caparisoned warrior-bird is not molting, as a friend of mine has suggested, but is collecting the narcotic fruit of the *ullucho* tree, which grows in the highlands. In contrast to the painted version, we illustrate a serenely simple Period IV modeled representation (65), once ornamented with inlays of stone or shell. It is identified as a hawk warrior only by its face, which may be either symbolic or an actual mask. Reality and unreality were often subtly blended by the Mochica, who made little distinction between the human and animal worlds, or literal and imaginative concepts.

OPPOSITE: 65

66

RUNNERS

Runners carrying bags of beans were another group important to the ceremonial life of the Mochica. Their basic costume was a belted loincloth and a special headdress featuring either a disk or a wedge-shaped ornament (66). Like the warriors, they were divided into classes associated with swift birds and animals that are often identified by face masks, and streamerlike wing and tail attributes attached to a strap anchored in the headdress and belt. A study of the many representations of runners in Mochica art suggests that ritual races were staged, involving destinations in various parts of the Mochica realm (indicated by landscape symbols), to deliver beans to priests for interpretation.

The significance of the beans is a subject of controversy among Peruvianists. Some are inclined to credit them with symbolic values by which elaborate messages could be conveyed. Their evident importance in warfare, as indicated by the representations of beans in the guise of warriors (67), tends to support this contention. Scenes of priests interpreting the beans, however, suggest that a form of divination was involved, which might be compared to the reading of tea leaves or palmistry. The beans may have been consulted for omens upon which to base military decisions, but it would seem that their most logical use would have involved predictions of agricultural fertility. The bean was one of the first domesticated plants in Peru (although in Mochica times the principal crop was maize), and its ritual importance may reflect the survival of traditions from a much earlier period. It is interesting to note that beans also played a major symbolic role in the iconography of the contemporary Nazca culture on the south coast of Peru.

67

MODES OF REPRESENTATION

The painted and modeled versions of Mochica warriors and runners offer us an opportunity to contrast the stylistic conventions of the two modes of representation. We have noted that the modeled pieces do not attempt to represent action and, for practical reasons, are compact in form. They are, however, essentially realistic, with components of the body and costume in their proper relationship to each other (68). The painted figures are rendered schematically, as in ancient Egyptian art, so that each element is seen from its most easily identifiable aspect (66). The head, arms, and legs are seen from the side, while the distinctive headdress ornaments, tunics, and tailpieces are shown from the front. The Mochica did not attempt to show perspective or spatial relationships. The size of the figures may sometimes indicate their importance, but is most often simply the result of their having been fitted to the available space.

Landscape settings are suggested symbolically. A wavy line often designates the ground (67), and shorthand elements, much like those of Minoan art, sometimes indicate sand, rock, or water. The locale, whether coastal or highland, desert or valley, is often indicated by placing plants, birds, and animals characteristic of these areas around the figures (69). The use of such background symbols as space fillers increases throughout the fourth period and often crowds the motif in the fifth.

[50]

68

69

70

RELIGION

The most dramatic evidence of cultural continuity on the north coast of Peru is the fact that the feline-fanged god of Chavín continued, with little change, as the principal deity of the Mochica (70) and their descendants, the Chimú, who, at the time of the Spanish conquest, referred to him as "Ai-Apec." Mochica ceramics in the Cummings collection give ample testimony to the tradition of his

71

72

73

highland origin. In one (71), he is seen emerging from a mountainside grotto, while two attendants stand by, holding the double-headed snake he wore as a belt; snails, which lived among the wet rocks and symbolized the locale, may be seen in relief on the slopes above. In other examples, Ai-Apec is shown against a background of mountain peaks that often resemble the form of a puma paw (72), or is seen supervising a human sacrifice on a mountaintop altar.

Perhaps the most interesting ceramic dealing with Ai-Apec is a model of a temple pyramid such as the Mochica built on the coastal plain, perhaps to represent the mountain home of their god (73). Snail shells edge the spiral ramp and highland pumas are painted on the walls. Near the top stand two figures, painted on the wall, one holding a bean bag and the other holding wands used in divination ceremonies. They appear to be delivering these to Ai-Apec, who is seated in the shrine above.

Ai-Apec was a warrior-god who fought all threats to the survival of his people. He was guardian of agriculture, of domestic animals, and of the food of

the sea. On an early painted vessel (75) he is seen aboard a balsa raft casting a weighted net to catch a skate. This scene suggests that, like the gods and cult heroes of many other peoples, he may also have been credited with the introduction of fishing and other vital skills.

The Mochica often gave minor deities the attributes of their god, a fact that makes some scenes of battle among the supernaturals difficult for us to interpret. For example, an unusual ceramic combining relief and sculpture in the round (74) represents a fight between Ai-Apec and a crab deity whose face and shell both bear the features of the god. Judging from the seals executed in relief between the combatants, the setting is the seashore. The subject is possibly a mythical encounter in which the god subdued the shore demon and won his cooperation. In another frequently depicted scene, an Ai-Apec crab is shown catching a fierce fish demon (31) on a hooked line, while it slashes at him with a chopperlike knife. The crab deity appears to be defending the sea against a force that would drive away the food on which the Mochica depended.

Fruits and vegetables important in the agricultural economy of the Mochica were often given deity or spirit attributes to symbolize their growth force or,

75

79

80

perhaps, their nutritive power. Ai-Apec is shown in the form of a yuca root (76); an anthropomorphic potato holds a digging stick (77); and an owl-eyed human head grows from the top of a squash (78). The Mochica seem to have regarded the owl, omnipresent in the fields and the enemy of mice, as a friendly guardian spirit of agriculture. The Maya thought of him as a spirit of darkness and the harbinger of death, while we associate the bird with wisdom. We must therefore beware of interpreting Mochica animistic symbols in terms of our own or another cultural heritage.

We must also assume that even the most easily recognizable subjects had a special symbolic meaning to their creators. This does not prevent us from delighting in such imaginative, Aesop-fable-like concepts as a seated deer holding its young in its arms (79). Its exact meaning may be lost to us, but the Mochica's zest for life and sense of oneness with nature is conveyed across the long barrier of time.

Aerial view of the Tschudi Group, an important sector of the extensive ruins of Chanchan, the Chimú capital, now being restored. The large rectangular depression was a reservoir

5 OTHER NORTH COAST STYLES

Detail of the adobe wall decorations found in the temple complex in the upper right-hand corner of the photograph above

Most of our knowledge of the archaeology of the north Peruvian coast has been derived from the study of materials from sites in the Chicama, Moche, and Virú valleys. We know little about the cultural and stylistic chronology of the large, important area that lies between the Mochica heartland and the Ecuadorian border. It includes several small valleys and three very extensive, well-watered ones, the Jequetepeque, Lambayeque, and Piura, which were all densely populated in ancient times and contain the ruins of extensive cities, featuring vast and elaborate temple complexes. This area was little affected by the Tiahuanaco-Wari culture, which seems to have been unable to dominate the coast further north than the Chicama. It acted as a reservoir of early local traditions, which reasserted themselves throughout the entire north coast after the collapse of the coastal Tiahuanaco empire in the formation of the powerful Chimú culture. The Chimú capital, Chanchan, in the Moche Valley near modern Trujillo, is the largest known metropolis of pre-Columbian America, and a model of enlightened city planning. After its conquest by the Inca in 1471, it continued to serve as the seat of government in the north coast, and remained to astound the Spanish conquistadors under Francisco Pizarro, who arrived sixty-one years later.

The long and complex history of the greater north coast area produced a bewildering diversity of ceramic styles. Much of the pottery was blackware, all of which has often been incorrectly lumped together under the term "Chimú." We have seen that black ceramics were used in early Chavinoid times and were brought to great heights by Mochica craftsmen. Many ceramics identified as Chimú are, in fact, contemporary with Mochica wares. An example is a stirrup-spout bottle (81), probably from the Lambayeque Valley, which is decorated in low relief with a battle between feline and fish demons. The style is very similar to that of Mochica relief pottery of the second period, and is probably contemporary. The feature of monkeys on the spout has commonly been considered diagnostic of Chimú ceramics, because they frequently appear in somewhat similar form beside the spouts of typically

83, 84

Chimú vessels. It is evident, however, that the motif was used in the period contemporary with the Mochica, and was but one of the many non-Mochica characteristics of earlier north coast styles that were continued or revived in Chimú times.

North coast blackware vessels sometimes have long, tapering spouts and broad, arched handles, features that are generally taken to indicate Tiahuanaco-Wari influence, as they are found throughout the coast in that period. The vessel illustrated as Figure 82, therefore, may be contemporary with the coastal Tiahuanaco culture; it comes from the far north area and has this kind of spout and handle. Its blind spout containing a whistle, in the form of a seated figure, is a variant of the trait that originated on the south coast, which we saw earlier, in Cupisnique, Salinar, and Gallinazo context. It evidently was diffused southward again during the coastal Tiahuanaco period. A crudely executed slip-painted double bottle with whistle from the central coast (83) indicates the decadence that overtook many of the areas conquered by the Tiahuanaco-Wari.

Many of the ceramic forms disseminated by the far-flung empire continued after its collapse. A blackware version of the same type of vessel (84) exhibits characteristic Chimú stylistic traits: the modeling is much simplified over Mochica examples, and the flasklike rear portion (84, right) is ornamented with typical Chimú "pressed" decoration, the texture and frontal figure being imparted by the

84

85

86

87

molds in which the piece was made. The front half is in the form of a cube, with a strange ritual scene on top. A seated figure holds a cup. Around him are gathered two frogs, a bird, and three human or monkey figures. (The head of the figure at front has been clumsily restored.)

Our most characteristic example of Chimú ware is a stirrup-spout vessel in the form of a crouching puma (85). The small monkey at the juncture of the long spout and the flattened stirrup are typical of ceramics of this culture. Though mass-produced, these pieces are often well made and fired, with highly polished, metallic-black surfaces. In comparison to Mochica realism, however, the modeling is greatly simplified.

Chimú ceramics changed little after the Inca conquest, except that in general they became more formal, and the spout sometimes was given a flaring rim (characteristic of Inca ceramics), like the example shown here (87), which also has a pressed band of birds and fish. Our final illustration, a double-chambered whistling vessel (86), also belongs to this late period. It portrays two figures carrying a covered funerary litter.

HIGHLAND INCA

Highland Inca ceramics tended to be austere and elegant in both form and ornamentation. A grave lot of undecorated miniature vessels from Cuzco (88) demonstrates some of their characteristic types. The most typical is a jar of the aryballos shape, used to contain liquids: it has two loop handles, a wide flaring lip at the top of its slim neck, and a conical base that facilitated pouring. These jars were often very large, as were the wide-mouthed jars with conical bases called *chicha* jars, since they were used to make a corn beer of that name. When vessels of either type were carried on the back, a rope was passed through the handles and secured around a lug supplied for this purpose. The Inca ceramic forms were so highly conventionalized that the lug was placed on all sizes of vessels, even the miniature ones shown here. Other characteristic forms appearing in this grave lot are a footed, loop-handled jar and shallow, saucerlike trays.

An unusual aryballoid jar (89) is decorated in a rare figurative style, with

88

89

circles containing stylized birds and flies against a background of flies and simplified monkeys. Though classic in form, it could have originated almost anywhere in the far-flung Inca empire.

CHANCAY-INCA

Contemporary with the north coast Chimú, a similar confederation was formed on the central coast, which is generally known by the name of one of its principal valleys, the Chancay. A typical ceramic type of this culture is a large, rather crude effigy vessel decorated in white and black (90). Chancay pottery continued with little change during the Inca period, although the Inca flaring lip sometimes appeared on spouts. It is seen, for instance, on a white double vessel (91), whose second spout is in the form of a human figure. There are simple, geometric designs painted in black and red-brown on the top of the vessel and on its flattened strap handle.

90

OPPOSITE: *Machu Picchu, the famous Inca city built on a mountain ridge high above the Urubamba Valley, south central Peru*

The ceramics and other craft products of the Chimú and Chancay cultures, while often possessing great charm and interest, never achieved the variety, technical brilliance, and artistic excellence that had been characteristic of Mochica times. Emphasis was less on craftsmanship than on mass production and the achievement of effect with a minimum of effort. The cultural advances of the late periods were mainly in the realms of city building, engineering, and social organization. The brief renewal of artistic excellence in the Inca period represented the sophisticated maturity of ancient Peruvian civilization, which never matched the creative vigor of its youth.

91

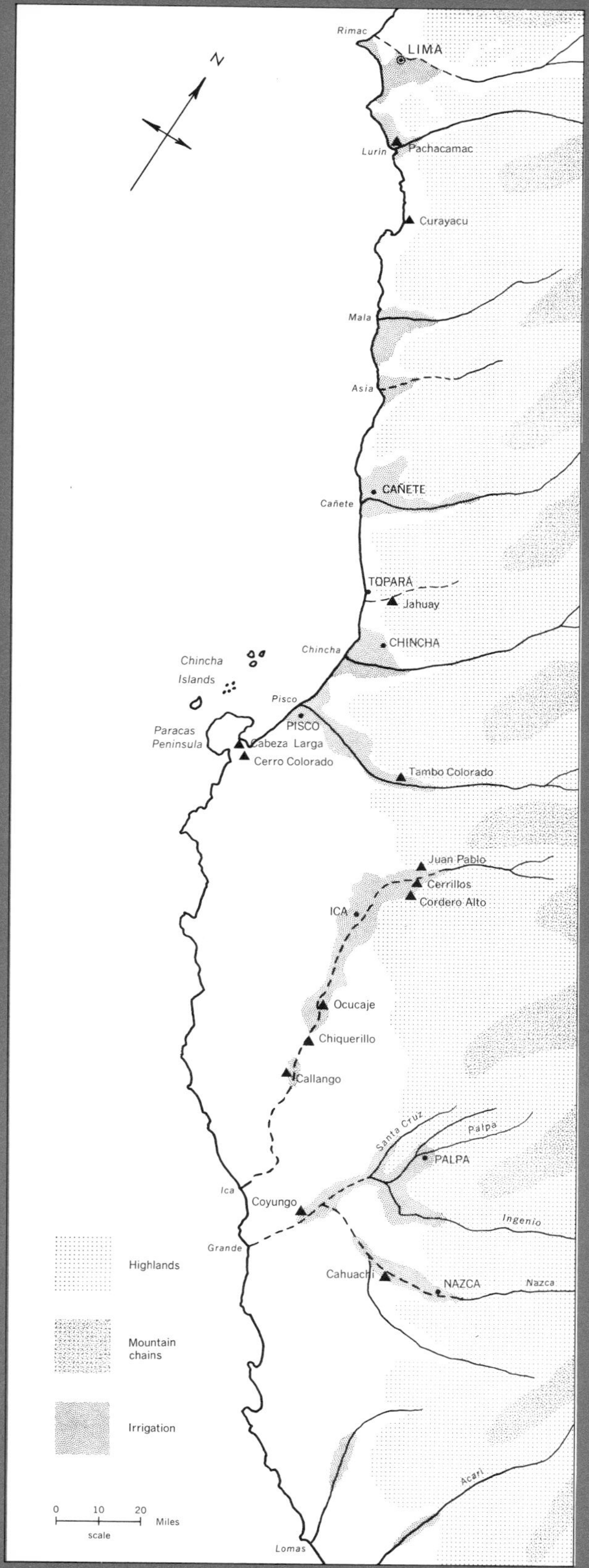

THE SOUTH COAST

Rimac
LIMA
Lurin Pachacamac

Curayacu

Mala

Asia

CAÑETE
Cañete

TOPARA
Jahuay

Chincha
Islands
Chincha CHINCHA

Pisco
PISCO
Cabeza Larga
Paracas
Peninsula
Cerro Colorado
Tambo Colorado

Juan Pablo
Cerrillos
Cordero Alto
ICA

Ocucaje

Chiquerillo

Callango

Santa Cruz Palpa
PALPA
Ingenio

Ica
Coyungo

Grande
Cahuachi NAZCA Nazca

Highlands

Mountain
chains

Irrigation

0 10 20 Miles
scale

Acari

Lomas

6 THE GREAT DISCOVERY

THE SUN-SCORCHED Paracas peninsula juts into the Pacific, forming a sheltered bay where the southern edge of the Pisco Valley meets the sea. The ruins of an ancient town lie swallowed in the sand, forming a long, almost imperceptible arc high above the beach. Nearby looms a hill called Cerro Colorado, multipeaked with outcroppings of red porphyry, and rose-tinted by thousands of small pebbles of the same material exposed on its windswept surface. Early in the century, industrious Peruvian treasure hunters called *huaqueros* began digging in this desolate place, and soon the fine textiles and other materials they found were appearing on the world's art markets. Then, in 1925, the famed Peruvian archaeologist Julio C. Tello traced the new finds to their source, and conducted extensive excavations that gave the Paracas culture its name and greatly enriched our knowledge of ancient Peruvian civilization.

On the crest of Cerro Colorado, the excavators discovered deep shaft tombs widened at the base to form chambers in which numerous burials had been placed. Concentrations of similar interments were found in pits of various dimensions in the nearby saddles of the hill. The contents of the tombs were in poor condition, but yielded geometrically decorated textile fragments woven in diverse techniques, and incised pottery colored with resinous paint after firing. Dr. Tello named the culture that produced them "Paracas Cavernas."

Beneath dusty sand and refuse filling the ruins of ancient buildings on the northern slope of Cerro Colorado, the excavators found a cache of several hundred large funerary bundles. Each consisted of a body in seated position wrapped in alternate layers of elaborately embroidered garments and plain cotton shrouds, interspersed with well-made but relatively undecorated pottery and a variety of other artifacts. The complete dryness of the area and the protection of the tomb fill had kept the magnificent textiles and other fragile materials in a remarkable state of preservation. With understandable enthusiasm over his fabulous discovery, Dr. Tello gave this group the somewhat extravagant cultural designation of "Paracas Necropolis."

The expedition uncovered other burials in the habitation site below, which had become known as "Cabeza Larga" due to the peculiar elongated skulls of the Paracas people, deformed by binding, which the huaqueros had left scattered about. The contents of tombs found here were classified according to the textile and ceramic types of the Cavernas and Necropolis graves.

Back at the National Museum of Archaeology and Anthropology in Lima, Dr. Tello and his co-workers turned to the painstaking and time-consuming job of carefully unwrapping some of the largest and most impressive Necropolis mummy bundles. They installed the contents dramatically in a central hall of the museum and soon their great discovery gained world renown. No burials have yet been found at other Paracas sites that approach the splendor of those in the Necropolis tombs of Cerro Colorado. This fact led Tello to suggest that the site was a repository for the funerary bundles of exceptionally important personages from the whole Paracas area. We still lack sufficient information to prove or disprove this interesting possibility.

In interpreting his Paracas finds Tello used his extraordinary knowledge of ancient Andean art styles, gained in years of exploration throughout the length and breadth of Peru. In certain of the pottery he assigned to Cavernas (including some from Ocucaje in the Ica Valley) he detected influence of the early, widespread Chavín horizon. Among the embroidered Necropolis textiles he found many bearing designs similar to those on Cavernas weaving, while others exhibited more naturalistic motifs closely resembling Nazca ceramic decoration. He therefore concluded that Cavernas was the older of the two phases he had discovered, and that the Paracas culture was post-Chavín and pre-Nazca and had flourished around the fifth century B.C. Present evidence indicates that Tello was substantially correct in these basic assumptions.

The history of the Paracas culture is now known to have been much longer and more complex than Tello and his co-workers could have realized. In the years following their discovery they and other Peruvianists made the logical mistake of trying to include incised pottery and non-embroidered textiles of all Paracas sites under the term "Cavernas," while "Necropolis" continued to encompass a diversity of non-incised ceramics and embroidered textiles of two distinct stylistic traditions. The two pigeonholes, particularly that of Cavernas, soon became uncomfortably overcrowded, and the original and proper meaning of Tello's terms obscured.

Sand dunes in the desert bordering the Ica Valley

The desolate Paracas peninsula, looking east from Cabeza Larga toward Cerro Colorado. A partly cleared house can be seen in the foreground

During the past twelve years archaeologists have investigated some of the manifestations of Paracas culture in each south coast valley from the Cañete to the Rio Grande de Nazca. Meanwhile, large collections of Paracas ceramics and textiles have been formed both in Peru and this country as the result of extensive clandestine digging carried out in the south coast, particularly in the Ica Valley. A detailed study of these materials in the light of the archaeological evidence now available enables us to reconstruct the broad trends in the development of Paracas culture. A long era of Chavín-influenced development preceded Tello's Cavernas period. I will divide this into a Formative Paracas period, in which Chavín influence was dominant, and an Early Paracas period, characterized by the florescence of regional styles growing out of the Formative style and perhaps with continuing, though diminished, Chavín influence. The Cavernas culture now appeared throughout the south coast, but since it affected these regional styles unequally I will refer to the period of its ascendancy as Middle Paracas. The time span covered by Tello's term "Necropolis" will be divided into the Late Paracas and Proto-Nazca periods.

The five divisions of Paracas culture are of unequal duration, but each has its own distinctive character, reflecting shifts in the major outside influences that contributed to its development (see the chronology chart on page 13). The interpretations advanced in the discussion that follows are my own, based on ten years of careful analysis of collections, coupled with field reconnaissance and stratographic excavations. They represent a slight modification of a chronology that I first published in 1961. Those interested in examining a somewhat different point of view are referred to the results of a parallel study conducted at the University of California, Berkeley, which was published by Menzel, Rowe, and Dawson in the fall of 1964. Only time and much more thorough archaeological spadework will clarify with absolute certainty the perplexing inter-relationships of diverse stylistic traditions that the Paracas sequence presents.

[71]

7 THE EARLY CERAMIC PERIOD

IN THOSE areas of the north and central coasts where Early Ceramic sites have been thoroughly studied, it has been found that a long period of cultural development preceded the arrival of Chavín influence around 900 B.C. In most cases, Early Ceramic technology was equal or superior to that of the Chavín culture, whose dynamic religion appears to have been the factor that brought about closer relationships between isolated valleys and an acceleration of cultural progress throughout most of Peru.

We do not yet fully understand the nature of the Early Ceramic period of the south coast. When we do, it will undoubtedly explain the presence of many non-Chavín forms and techniques in the ceramics of the earliest Paracas periods. These include the distinctive double-spout and bridge-handled bottle, with one spout blind, modeled, and often containing a whistle. Also present are the occasional use of oxidation firing, red slip, and negative decoration. The technique of applying resin paints after firing seems, like incised decoration, to have been widespread in the Early Ceramic period and its probable point of origin has not yet been determined.

One curious ceramic in the Cummings collection, said to have come from Chiquerillo, a small early site between Ocucaje and Callango, may belong to the pre-Chavinoid period (92). Certainly it is very primitive and falls outside the range of any known Paracas style. It is a dull brown, semioxidized vessel with a single spout and two modeled animal heads. The sides are daubed with blotches of heavy red slip.

92

93

8 THE FORMATIVE PARACAS PERIOD

THE PARACAS culture began with the establishment of strong Chavín influence in the south coast valleys, particularly, it would seem from present evidence, in the Ica. The source of this influence, as well as the route by which it arrived and was sustained, is still a matter of speculation. Presumably the center from which it spread was in the northern highlands, an area separated from the south coast by about four hundred miles of rugged mountains and barren coastal desert. The fact that Chavinoid ceramics have been discovered at several points along the intervening coast has led to the assumption that influence flowed southward, valley by valley, but nowhere did a florescence of culture result comparable to what took place in the Paracas area. It therefore seems possible that the influence may have traveled a more direct highland or sea route, and that the south coast valleys possessed a relatively advanced Early Ceramic culture particularly receptive to Chavín stimulation.

Most of the Chavinoid Paracas ceramics now available for study have derived from huaquero activity in the Callango area, which lies in the southern part of the Ica Valley near the sea. A few of these are so like Chavín types that Peruvianists have suggested that they might be imports from the north coast or high-

94, 95

lands. Other Chavinoid materials have been found at Paracas sites throughout
the valley. The earliest levels so far scientifically studied were excavated by
Dwight T. Wallace at Cerrillos in the upper Ica, but judging from the total range
of style they fall at least midway in the Formative period.

A small group of ceramics in the Cummings collection, said to have come
from Chiquerillo, shows a considerable range of early traits. The piece most like
Chavín and Early Cupisnique wares and, therefore, apparently the oldest and pre-
Cerrillos in date, is a well-polished, thick-walled blackware beaker with a pouring
lip on its beveled rim (93). The sides are decorated with a chevron pattern incised
in broad lines that were filled with resin-based paints. The pattern was omitted
beneath the lip, for liquids spilled while pouring would tend to endanger the pigments. This seems to explain why gaps were left in the design on most subsequent Paracas bowls, though the pouring lip itself disappeared by the end of the
Formative period.

95

96

A grave lot of two bowls with well-preserved resinous paint shows several typical traits of the Cerrillos time range. One (94), hemispherical in form, is decorated with a band of figure-eights executed with reed sections of two different diameters. Both the reed-stamped circle and the guilloche are motifs common in Chavín art and were to be among the most persistent of Paracas design elements. The lack of pouring lip on this bowl indicates that it was used for food rather than for liquids. The second piece in the grave lot (95) is a straight-sided bowl decorated with an incised and painted human face with a characteristic Chavinoid treatment of the eye, as can be seen by comparing it to the figure on a stone relief at Chavín de Huántar (96). The representation is evidently of a human being rather than an anthropomorphic feline deity since the mouth lacks the god's feline fangs. Circles, without incisions, have been painted on the remainder of the sides, except below the pouring lip.

Three late Formative period ceramics from Chiquerillo illustrate motifs that were to play a major role in the Early Paracas period that followed. The first is a double-spout bottle (97) with one spout capped with a bird head, painted red, that contains a whistle vented below the beak. Incised on the body of the vessel

97

98

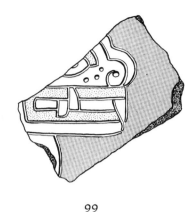

99

is a frontal feline mask with characteristic late Chavinoid conventionalization of the eyes and the mouth, which exhibits overlapping fangs. On this bottle, as is often the case with Paracas ceramics, the resinous paint has deteriorated so that only the red can be positively identified. With the exception of red and a very few other earth colors, most of the pigments seem to have contained soluble dyes that were leached out by ground water, for all that is left when they have broken down is the whitish residue of the matrix.

In Chavín art the feline is usually shown as a full figure with both the body and the head in profile (98), but profile feline heads do not occur on Paracas ceramics, except for rare occurrences in the Formative period, an example being the design on a sherd I found at Juan Pablo in 1960 (99). The profile seems to have been avoided to prevent confusion between the snub-nosed feline and the longer-snouted fox, a motif that was of special importance on the south coast. The Paracas frontal version was either a variation of the Chavín anthropomorphic feline-deity head or, more likely, a composite of two profiles face to face. The frontal feline mask bottle — without a whistle in the spout, though the red bird head with vent remains — became characteristic of the Juan Pablo style throughout the remainder of the Paracas sequence.

What may be an early version of the fox motif appears on our next example, a lenticular bowl with incised and resin-painted designs over its entire top surface (100). Two panels contain abstract profile heads with a foreleg extended under and in front of the jaw. This design would be interpreted as feline if it

100

were not for the fact that the elongated mouth with foreleg below are features of later renderings readily identifiable as the fox. (The distinction between fox and feline will become clear as we trace the motifs through subsequent Paracas periods.) The heads alternate with panels of diamond designs enclosing an eye pattern. The latter is one of the most characteristic Chavín symbols (one might compare it to the early Christian "eye of God") that occurs frequently in the following Early Paracas period.

101, 102

103

Our final Chavinoid example from Chiquerillo is an unusual two-lobed form with a spout at one end, a modeled bird head containing a whistle on the other, and a bridge handle between (101). The legs, wings, and tail of the bird are incised and painted on the body of the vessel below the head, and a Chavín eye pattern is painted, without incised lines, on each side. The eared head, in this case, resembles an owl, but on a slightly later Juan Pablo version shown for comparison (102) a similar head has bands extending below and behind each eye, a marking that in both Chavín and Paracas art is an identifying trait of the falcon. Though whistle-spout bottles are common in the Formative period, this is the only type that continues in Early Paracas, where it occurs at Juan Pablo and Callango. Its rarity suggests a special use in ritual. As I mentioned earlier, similar whistle bottles appeared later in north coast negative-horizon styles (a Gallinazo version is shown in Figure 103). Exactly why and how the trait migrated we do not know, but the whistle spout continued to occur in various cultures down through the Inca period, giving it a known time span of over two thousand years.

The Paracas site of Pinilla, at Ocucaje. In the foreground are open tombs left by huaqueros

I have placed the end of the Formative period of the Paracas culture at the somewhat arbitrary point where Chavín influence on the south coast appears to have lost its dominant role and distinctive local ceramic styles emerged. Of all the Paracas centers in the Ica, Ocucaje, in the central part of the valley, was the most responsive to outside influence. We will therefore trace the development of its ceramic style through the remaining Paracas periods before turning to the more conservative Juan Pablo and Callango styles.

9 THE OCUCAJE EARLY PARACAS STYLE

THE FIRST phase of the Early Paracas style at Ocucaje is well represented by a grave lot of thirteen ceramics (104). As a group they show a refinement of Formative types and motifs. They are remarkable in their consistent small size, fine workmanship, and matching color scheme, in which a carbon-blackened body is set off by designs in resinous paints of red, yellow, green, and dark brown, with minor accents of light and dark yellow and dark olive green. The vessels also share identical iconographic elements. Their association is therefore probably valid, although the grave was not scientifically excavated.

One of the most interesting pieces is a feline effigy jar (106), from which all traces of paint, except for the red, have disappeared, a loss that is said to have been caused by its having been placed in the hands of the body in the tomb. The treatment of the motif is quite Chavinoid, especially in the handling of the eyes,

104

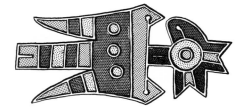

105

106

107

the fanged mouth, and the whiskers, which curl from the ends of the mouth as they do on the Chiquerillo bottle (97). The rendering is, however, more detailed and precise. The double-circle pelt marking, another early trait, is shared by three other pieces in the grave lot. Three more have circles without incisions, a device we have already seen on a late Formative period bowl (95).

Another unusual and attractive ceramic is a small double-spout bottle, with resin-painted decoration over its entire top surface featuring a bird design (105). This motif is sometimes identified as a male condor, with the projection above the head interpreted as the comb peculiar to that species. It does not, however, bear any significant resemblance to the Chavín rendering of the bird (3), which has a profile feline head with condor beak and comb affixed to the front. Although the

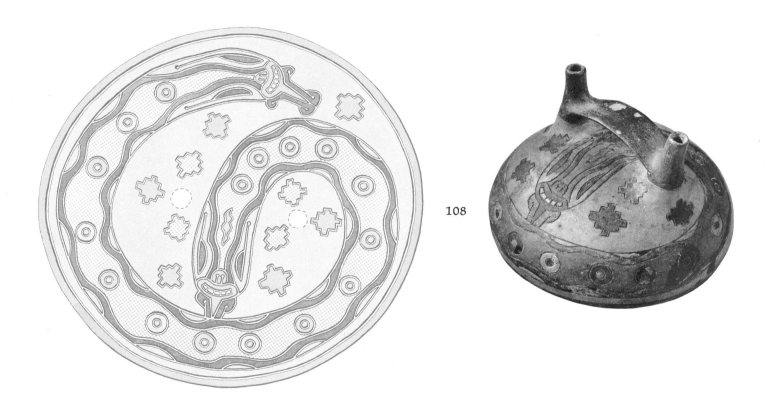

108

condor interpretation cannot be ruled out, I am inclined to believe that the motif does not occur in Paracas iconography of the Ica Valley, but is replaced by the locally more important falcon. The eye marking diagnostic of the falcon may be represented in this version by the inner bands on the two double-pointed projections. This identification will be further supported when we examine the more realistic renderings of the falcon in the Middle Paracas period at Ocucaje, as well as in related versions from Juan Pablo and Callango.

The final ceramic of this grave lot worthy of special attention is a pitcherlike jar with a broad strap handle, bearing a double-headed serpent motif (107). Formative period precedents for this motif, as well as for the vessel's shape, are

109

known, and the double-headed serpent remains important in Ocucaje iconography throughout the Paracas sequence. For comparative purposes a second example of this design is illustrated (108), which ornaments a double-spout bottle from a more or less contemporary grave. Both snakes have feline noses and pelt markings — an example of an important characteristic of Chavín art: the endowment of all religious symbols with feline attributes. As we shall see later when we examine Callango ceramics, in modeled versions of the same period, double-headed serpents not only have these attributes but catlike ears as well. It follows that the similar ears of falcon-head spouts are also feline in inspiration.

Two double-spout bottles, both featuring feline figure motifs, illustrate the continuity and gradual change of the Early Paracas style at Ocucaje. The smaller one (109) has more advanced traits than the feline effigy jar of the grave lot. The head and figure have been greatly simplified, and the features of the face reduced to geometric elements. The mouth occupies the width of the head, and though it retains its fangs, they no longer protrude beyond the lip in the Chavinoid manner. Whiskers now appear as appendages below the chin, forecasting a trend that continues throughout the remainder of the Paracas sequence at Ocucaje.

The larger bottle (110) has two open spouts, one ornamented with a falcon head, and a bowl-shaped base bearing a geometric design. The feline figure is similar to the other example except for the mouth, which has been shortened and lacks fangs. It would appear to represent a later phase of the Early Paracas period than those previously discussed, since the treatment of the mouth is closely related to that of the following, Middle Paracas period.

110

10 THE OCUCAJE MIDDLE PARACAS STYLE

THE EARLY Paracas period came to an end when the Cavernas culture moved into the south coast valleys, bringing about a cultural and stylistic revolution at those centers it dominated, as sweeping as that initiated by Chavín influence centuries before. Like Chavín, Cavernas influence was most evident in the realm of religious concepts and was reflected in a radically new iconography.

The Cavernas group introduced a trophy-head cult with elaborate human, monkey, and feline deities, having serpentine appendages and carrying trophy heads and triangular knives. (The actual knives, found in graves, are made of obsidian, with wooden handles bound on with gut.) These motifs soon dominated the decoration of Ocucaje textiles and ceramics, making them almost indistinguishable from those Tello found in Cavernas graves on the Paracas peninsula. Strangely enough, upper valley centers such as Juan Pablo did not accept the new cult, but continued with their Early Paracas symbols only slightly modified by the influence of the dynamic new group. In the southern part of the valley, at Callango, the new ideas and motifs were accepted with reservations and rendered side by side with traditional ones on pottery essentially Early Paracas in form.

Cavernas-influenced Ocucaje textile motifs are usually highly geometricized, with designs reduced to vertical, horizontal, and diagonal components, in the tradition of such techniques as gauze and double cloth. In ceramics, on the other hand, the precise geometrical drawing of the Early Paracas style gave way to a bolder, more dynamic, freehand manner, closely related to that used on pyroengraved gourds. A characteristic Cavernas-style gourd is illustrated here (111). The two

111

112

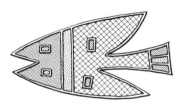

monkey deities ornamenting the exterior are rendered in curving lines, except for sawtooth elements on the back that correspond to textile versions. The interior bears a human figure whose round head is surrounded by hairlocks, and a band of stylized cats borders the rim. (This, by the way, is the only decorated gourd in the Cummings collection, but the art form is probably the oldest of the Andean area. It originated in remote pre-ceramic times and is still practiced today.)

Middle Paracas, Cavernas-influenced pottery was decorated with the same type of incisions and resin-based paints that had been used in the Formative and Early Paracas periods. The forms of the vessels, however, shifted abruptly from the neat, gambreled bowls and bottles of Early Paracas to less sophisticated and rather crudely polished shapes with hemispherical bases.

A spectacular ceramic drum (112) sums up the new style. Two large monkey figures on the sounding chamber illustrate typical traits of Cavernas trophy-head-cult deities: bulging eyes, grinning mouths with the tongue protruding below the chin, cheeks sprouting whisker symbols, and triangular knives appended to the head and held in the hand. The fangs that appear here, however, are unusual in Middle Paracas iconography. The two birds between the figures represent a Cavernas-influenced rendering of the falcon. The point of the drum is decorated with two abstract *vencejos*, whippoorwill-like birds that, like the fox, seem to have been of special local importance on the south coast. Though the motif is not found in Chavín art, it occurs in all Paracas and Nazca periods. This version, in which the head is shown as two triangles attached to the wing, is a typical Cavernas stylization of the vencejo.

Another type of Middle Paracas trophy-head deity is found on a wide-mouthed, keg-shaped jar that has abstract faces incised and painted on each side (113). The mouth with protruding tongue has whiskers curling from its corners, and the round, concave eyes are framed by horseshoe-shaped bands and an outer

114

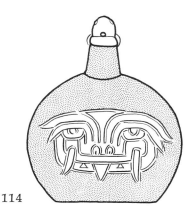

113

[85]

border from which triangular serpent heads project. This particular deity face is frequently found on Cavernas double-cloth textiles, as well as painted cotton masks that were placed over the head of Middle and Late Paracas mummy bundles at Ocucaje, but are evidently not found at Paracas peninsula sites.

Tello suspected that the Cavernas culture had Chavín origins. He may have been right, but, if so, the style evolved independently from any known to have existed in the south coast area. I have seen only one Chavinoid ceramic from the Ica Valley that shows a precedent for the grinning mouth and protruding tongue of the Cavernas deities: it is a double-spout bottle with whistle from Chiquerillo, in the collection of Mr. and Mrs. Raymond Wielgus (114). It came from the same source as the Cummings Paracas collection, and is said to have been found in a Chiquerillo grave with the beaker having a pouring lip and chevron design (Figure 93, our first illustration of Formative Paracas ceramics). The mask on the Wielgus bottle is close to Chavín in style, but at the same time suggests a proto-

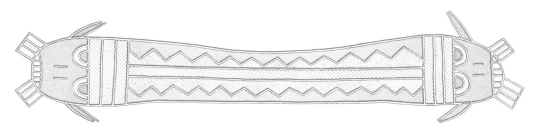

115

type for the jack-o'lantern-like Cavernas deity. The trophy-head cult, however, is a non-Chavinoid trait that must have been acquired and developed at some point on the independent route traveled by the Cavernas culture on its way to the south coast. Its area of origin is unknown, but because of the importance of the monkey motif, some intermountain valley in the highlands or the eastern slope of the Andes has been suspected.

In the Middle Paracas period at Ocucaje, familiar Early Paracas motifs such as the feline, the double-headed snake, and the falcon are rendered in a new, bold, freehand style that often combines the conventions of both traditions. A good example of this is a feline effigy jar with a double-headed serpent incised on its body (115). This ceramic, like our earlier example of similar form, was found in the hands of a burial, which accounts for the deterioration of much of its paint. The eyes, mouth, and whiskers of both feline and serpent heads follow the conventions of Cavernas feline trophy-head deities, and the zigzag markings on the back of the serpent parallel the outlines of figures on contemporary textiles.

Two simple feline figures incised on the interior of a hemispherical bowl follow Cavernas textile-design conventions even more closely, in the protruding tongue and the positioning of the tail above the back (116). A similar bowl bears a falcon design rendered in the same broad freehand style (117). The vertical bar marking extends both above and below the eye, as it often did in Early Paracas renderings, but the head is otherwise more naturalistic. The configuration of the wings and tail is similar to earlier versions. The rectangular body markings of both feline and falcon, as well as the reverse-repeat geometric motif on the sides of each bowl, are characteristic Middle Paracas motifs.

116

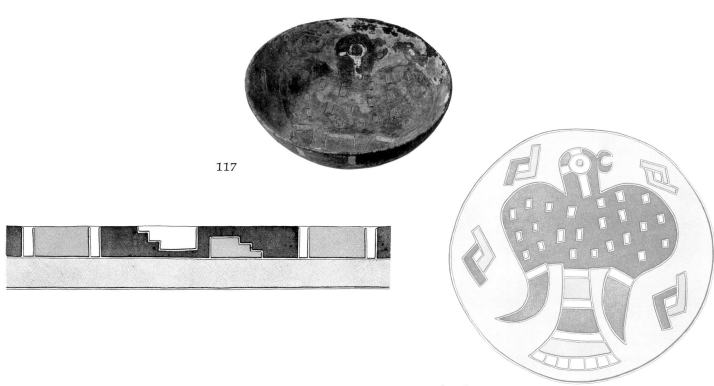

117

11 A RE-EXAMINATION OF "NECROPOLIS"

118

Before discussing the final and most complicated phases of the Paracas ceramic sequence at Ocucaje, it would be well for us to re-examine briefly the materials included under Tello's term "Necropolis." The relatively plain but well-made ceramics he found with Necropolis burials included two closely related stylistic groups, whose technology was completely different from that of Cavernas. At the same time many of the elaborately embroidered textiles that accompanied them were decorated with motifs closely related to those found on woven Cavernas fabrics, while others manifested a radically different style that was more naturalistic.

A mantle border in the Cummings collection is a fine example of the Cavernas-related Necropolis style (118). It bears a reverse-repeat of a complex monkey figure with long serpentine tail and similar head ornament, each having saw-tooth edges and ending with a trophy head like the one held in its hand. A larger trophy head is pendent to the chin, and within the body is a cat or monkey figure, which in turn contains a small feline. Small human, animal, and bird figures are used as background space fillers. Though the design is executed in embroidery and more elaborate, the figures conform to the rigid warp-and-weft controlled conventions of earlier woven renderings of the same cult deities.

Two obvious questions present themselves: first, where did the Necropolis tradition with its different ceramic and textile technology come from; and second, why did it then adopt new pottery forms and textiles bearing naturalistic embroideries, which relate more closely to the iconography of the post-Paracas, Nazca ceramic style? Recent archaeological investigations provide hints to possible answers.

The Necropolis ceramics of Cerro Colorado and Cabeza Larga in the Pisco Valley are almost identical with those of a culture called Topará in the Chincha and Cañete, the next two valleys to the north. Investigations conducted in this area by Louis M. Stumer, Edward P. Lanning, and Dwight T. Wallace have shown that the technique of oxidation firing had remained dominant there from pre-Chavinoid times (in contrast to the valleys to the south, where Paracas pottery showed a preference for semireduced carbon-blackened wares like those of Chavín). The Topará period, which followed what they call the Pozuelo and Patos periods (roughly equivalent to our Formative and Early Paracas), was characterized by thin, well-fired orange ware having simple shapes, sometimes covered with cream slip but with relatively little decoration. On the slim evidence of a few fragments of embroidered textiles found in early levels of this culture, and one piece of a pyroengraved gourd from a late level (119), it appears that Topará was a local variant of the Cavernas culture. If this is so, then the Cavernas-related phase of Necropolis could be explained as an expansion of the Topará people southward, establishing themselves as an élite group on the Paracas peninsula.

To understand the change that took place in the Necropolis (Toparoid?) style, once it had become established in the Pisco Valley, we must examine contemporary developments in the Rio Grande de Nazca area about a hundred miles to the southeast. These have been dramatically revealed by stratigraphic excavations conducted at Cahuachi by William Duncan Strong in 1952 and 1953. He discovered a chronological series of levels, which he divided into three phases, Late Paracas, Proto-Nazca, and Early Nazca. Although a wide variety of ceramic types was encountered, the three phases together showed a smooth transition from Paracas to Nazca decorative techniques. The most significant shift was from incised and resin-painted wares in Late Paracas to incised and polychrome slip-painted ceramics in Proto-Nazca, and finally, in Early Nazca, to pottery decorated with colored slips but without incisions.

At first glance, the technically superior Late Paracas wares of Cahuachi resemble the Cavernas ceramics we have seen from Ocucaje. There are, however, important stylistic and iconographic differences. At Cahuachi, drawing is more naturalistic and controlled, and non-Cavernas motifs such as killer whales, fish, birds, animals, fruits, and vegetables appear together with modified trophy-head-cult deities. Associated textiles show these new motifs rendered naturalistically in embroidery. The contrast with Cavernas increased steadily throughout the Proto-Nazca phase until, in Early Nazca, trophy-head-cult iconography was merged with and dominated by a new cult of agricultural fertility.

119

We lack sufficient information on earlier phases of the Paracas culture in the Rio Grande de Nazca area to determine the origins of this unusual iconography. It may have developed locally in its Cavernas-influenced Middle Paracas period. On the other hand, it is possible that the new motifs derived from another, as yet unidentified source. It is also difficult to ascertain to what extent the southward spread of Necropolis influence may have stimulated the technological experimentation that led to the development of the Nazca polychrome-slip ceramic style. There is, however, ample evidence to demonstrate that this distinctive Paracas culture of the Rio Grande area exerted a strong counterwave of influence northward, which dominated the final phase of Paracas culture in the Ica Valley and carried it over into the Nazca period. At the same time it appears to have caused the Necropolis people of the Pisco Valley to adopt its naturalistic embroidery style and iconography and to modify their austere Toparoid ceramic tradition.

If my interpretation of the limited evidence at hand is correct, we have traced to their sources the contrasting stylistic traditions that reacted with the Cavernas tradition in the Late Paracas period at Ocucaje. For the sake of clarity we will need to define and limit the terms used to designate them. "Necropolis" will be limited to its Toparoid, Cavernas-related context, and "Rio Grande" will be used to designate the southern tradition (indicating Strong's Late Paracas phase at Cahuachi). I will use the term "Proto-Nazca" as Strong intended it — a technologically transitional phase between Late Paracas and Early Nazca.

120

12 THE LATE PARACAS PERIOD AT OCUCAJE

IN THE Late Paracas period at Ocucaje three distinct, though related, traditions — the local Cavernas, and the intrusive Necropolis and Rio Grande — competed for ascendancy. Each had its own craft technology, style conventions, and iconography, and the resulting coexistence and intermingling produced a profusion of ceramic types and decorative techniques difficult to relate to each other chronologically. We can only observe that the Rio Grande Paracas tradition soon gained a dominant position and that the Ocucaje style finally followed that of Cahuachi in its transition to Nazca. Individual pieces within technically related groups can be classified according to the influences they manifest and their relative position in the overall trend. To illustrate this point, let us consider several typical Late Paracas incised and resin-painted ceramics from Ocucaje.

A large Cavernas-type subglobular bottle has a blind spout in the form of a human head, and a frontal figure incised below on the body of the vessel (120). Highly conventionalized feline figures of the trophy-head cult are drawn on each side. The shape of the cat's head, triangular-knife appendage, and protruding

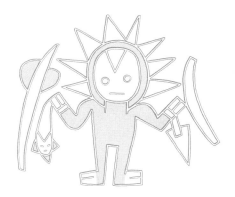

121

120, 121

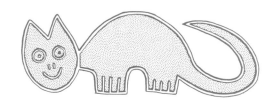

122

tongue, the leg treatment, and the zigzag border to the back and tail, as well as the serpent head terminating the tail, are all features that belong to neither the Cavernas nor Rio Grande stylistic conventions, but may be correlated with Necropolis textile renderings. The simplified treatment of the human figure and, in particular, the coffee-bean eyes of the head show Rio Grande influence.

A similar bottle, with head spout featuring coffee-bean eyes and a turban, has frontal human figures enclosed within a rainbow-like arc on the sides (121). This motif is sometimes found together with other figures wearing a winged forehead ornament peculiar to the Rio Grande tradition.

Double-based bowls with pellets between the bases to make them rattle are also a distinctive Rio Grande innovation. One from Ocucaje has a trophy-head deity rendered on its interior and simplified cat figures on its exterior sides (122). Both the felines and the deity are rendered in precise, flowing lines and are much more simplified than their Cavernas and Necropolis equivalents. The frequency of trophy-head-cult deities in the Rio Grande style suggest that the motif played a major role in its own Cavernas-influenced Middle Paracas period. The Cummings collection includes a varied group of these deities (124-128) ornamenting the sides of deep Late Paracas bowls (a characteristic Rio Grande shape).

The final phase of the Late Paracas style is neatly summarized by a grave lot from Ocucaje consisting of fourteen thin and beautifully fashioned ceramics of matching workmanship and color scheme (129). Four bowls have the hemispherical shape and decoration of baskets. A deep bowl with typical Rio Grande form is ornamented with triangular obsidian-knife motifs, another with engaging monkey figures, and a third has evenly spaced indentations outlined in leaflike shapes. Three more bowls have pinched sides, giving the rim a rounded square contour. One is decorated with S-shaped double-headed snakes, while the other two bear

123

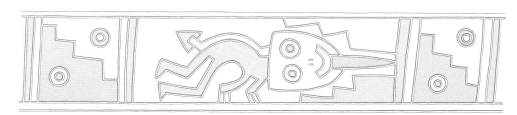

124

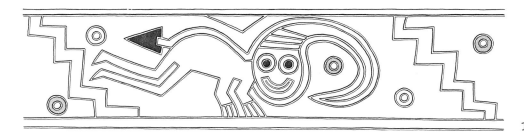

125

126

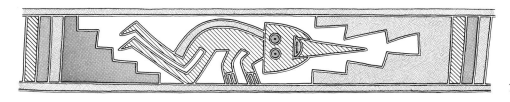

127

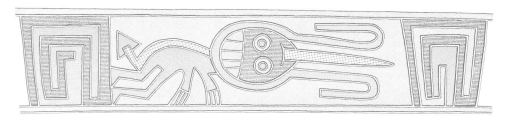

128

129

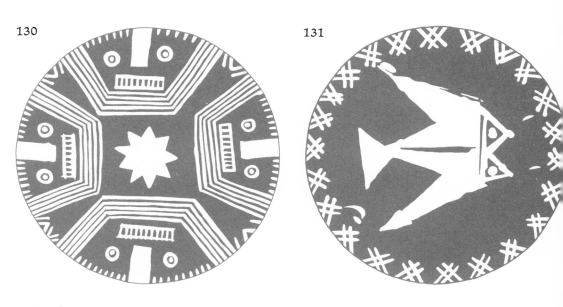

130
131

naturalistic killer-whale motifs. Two pairs of miniature jars in the form of feet are decorated with similar killer whales, together with simplified trophy-head demons (123). All the decoration is rendered in flowing lines of studied simplicity.

The trophy-head deities, the double-headed snakes, and the triangular knives are motifs shared by the Cavernas, Necropolis, and Rio Grande traditions. The killer-whale and monkey renderings, however, are singularly Rio Grande in origin, as are the forms, technology, and elegant execution of all the pieces.

Wares decorated in the negative technique with nonrepresentational patterns are characteristic of all Paracas periods in the Ica Valley, but none exhibit pictorial motifs until the Rio Grande-influenced, Late Paracas period. These negative designs usually ornament the interior of shallow bowls. Many of the subjects stem from the Cavernas tradition and are rendered in a rather angular style. Examples are simplified figures and heads of trophy-head-cult deities (130) and geometricized serpents and birds such as the vencejo shown here (131). Other bowls feature distinctive Rio Grande motifs, such as killer whales (132), fish (133), and simplified monkey figures (134).

129

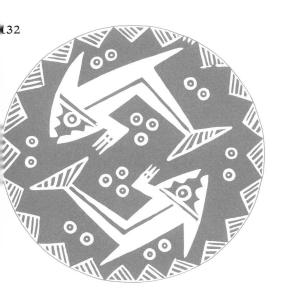

132

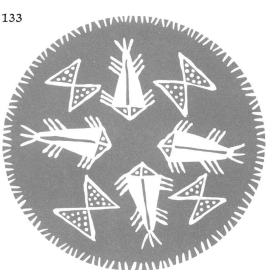

133

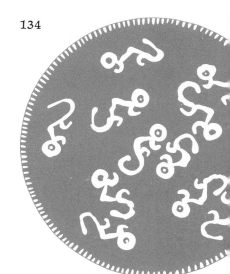

134

[95]

135, 136, 137, 138

13 THE PROTO-NAZCA PERIOD

In 1960 I conducted a stratigraphic cut in habitation refuse at a Paracas site on the Hacienda Cordero Alto in the upper Ica Valley just below Cerrillos. The excavation confirmed what Dr. Strong had found at Cahuachi — that the time range of stylistic types overlapped, and the assignment of a period designation to any given level was a matter of percentage. The transition from Late Paracas to Proto-Nazca and finally Early Nazca was smooth and gradual without any abrupt change.

The ceramic fragments encountered in my upper levels were predominantly Proto-Nazca types, such as fine black wares decorated in a variety of ways, and orange and buff wares ornamented by the negative technique, simple lines of cream and red slip, or incising and polychrome-slip painting. There were also a surprising number of Late Paracas incised and resin-painted sherds, as well as bottle and bowl fragments of the cream-slipped Necropolis type. The proportion of Proto-Nazca to Late Paracas sherds gradually reversed as deeper levels were encountered. Finally the Late Paracas ceramics, influenced by the Necropolis and Rio Grande styles, abruptly terminated as Middle Paracas levels were reached. I will discuss the upper Ica style in detail later when we examine Juan Pablo ceramics; the point I wish to make here is that the coexistence of diverse styles in the Late Paracas and Proto-Nazca periods makes exact chronological ordering all but impossible. The distinction between the two periods is as arbitrary, and at the same time necessary, as the division between Formative and Early Paracas.

[96]

Because of their technical affinity, Necropolis ceramics have often been equated with the Proto-Nazca style. This, I suspect, has been largely due to the fact that examples chosen to illustrate the Necropolis style have usually been selected from the more attractive Proto-Nazca-influenced types, such as Tello found in his late Necropolis burials with Nazca-like embroideries. A classic example of this type, truly a masterpiece of ceramic art, is a double-spout bottle with a capped, low ovoid body, which is gadrooned to resemble a pumpkin (139). This was found at Ocucaje.

Similar but less elaborate capped bottles are typical of Toparoid ceramics, and many variants are found at Ocucaje in the Late Paracas period. Two are illustrated: one with red slip (137) and the other with negative decoration (138).

There are many "Necropolis" cream-slipped bottles found at both Paracas peninsula sites and Ocucaje in the form of vegetables, birds, and animals. These most logically belong to the agricultural iconography of the Proto-Nazca period. Our Ocucaje example is a monkey effigy holding a fruit to its mouth (140). The

139, 140

141, 142

143

detail of the hands was incised and the eyes reed-stamped. The Cummings collection also contains several beautifully fashioned, unadorned, thin orange ware bottles with flaring spouts. They may represent Proto-Nazca precedents for the modified Necropolis types with naturalistic forms. We illustrate one with a realistic pumpkin shape (135) and another in the form of four bottle gourds (136). The flaring-spout type never has the Necropolis (Toparoid) cap, and it appears to be regional to the Ica and Rio Grande valleys.

While the Rio Grande de Nazca was the center for the development of the Nazca polychrome-slip ceramic tradition, a large number of transitional potteries

are found at Ocucaje. Two double-spout bottles, of modified Necropolis types, show an early stage of this trend. One is of highly fired gray-buff ware (141), with thick layers of cream-colored kaolin slip applied to its sides to form profile figures of felines, whose heads are rendered in high relief in the same material. The features of the heads are incised, as are the details of the paws. Another example is a bottle of similar ware with a strongly modeled fox-head blind spout (142). The teeth, nostrils, and whiskers are indicated with bold, incised lines and the eyes were executed with two reed stamps, forming concentric circles, and have deep punched dots in their centers. A band of heavy cream slip was applied along the ridge of the snout and the top of the head, and another, outlined by incisions, indicates the forelegs on the body of the vessel. A T-shaped element in cream slip indicates the tail at the back of the vessel. (The fox motif, which was absent from Early and Middle Paracas iconography at Ocucaje, was reintroduced with the Rio Grande style.) This interesting effigy bottle was found in the same grave as a Proto-Nazca blackware bowl with highly polished sides and a naturalistic bird drawn in burnished line on its matte interior (143).

Perhaps the most characteristic Proto-Nazca example in the Cummings collection is a double-spout bottle, globular in shape with a modified Necropolis-type capped top (144). A monkey trophy-head deity in low relief, outlined by incisions, is wrapped around the body of the vessel with the head projecting to one side. Many traits of this deity — the flowing line, almond-shaped eye, and winged forehead ornament — are diagnostic of the Proto-Nazca tradition. The forehead ornament and the circular disks at the sides of the face later became important features of Early Nazca iconography, and were frequently represented in the realistic Nazca-like embroideries from Paracas Necropolis. The most unusual feature of this vessel is, however, the fact that the colors were entirely rendered in slip,

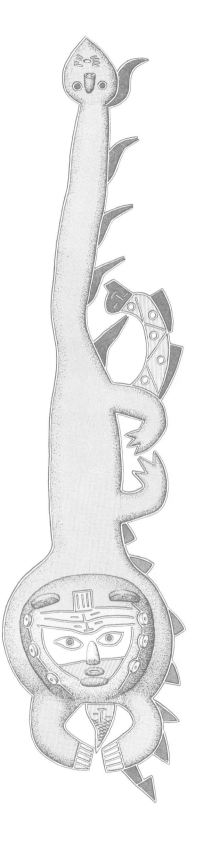

144

consisting of thin mixtures of clay containing mineral pigments that fired to Indian red, brownish black, gray, and cream over the orange body.

Our final Proto-Nazca example, a monkey effigy bottle with a strap handle leading from the head to the single spout (145), is much more advanced than the simple cream-slipped version we illustrated earlier (140). The figure is more realistically modeled; the color areas are outlined by incision and toned with dark red, olive gray, grayish cream, and black-brown slip. Although some features, such as the reed-stamped eyes, are conservative, the figure needs only to lose its incised lines to become Early Nazca in style. We will return to examine Nazca ceramics following our discussion of the Paracas styles of Juan Pablo and Callango.

145

The cemetery from which most of the Cummings Juan Pablo ceramics came, located between the foot of Cerro Teojate and the deeply undercut bank of the Ica River

14 THE JUAN PABLO STYLE

ABOUT FIFTY kilometers north of Ocucaje and fifteen above the city of Ica, the valley narrows as mountain spurs meet the coastal plain. The Juan Pablo cemeteries are located at the foot of Cerro Teojate, which rises close to the river's western bank at this point. The burials have been subject to ground water at various times in the past two thousand years: the colored pigments, originally much like those of Ocucaje, have deteriorated for the most part to powdery residue, and all perishable materials, such as textiles, have disappeared. Ancient habitation sites cover the steep slopes of the nearby hills and those across the valley, where the Cerrillos site excavated by Dr. Wallace and the Hacienda Cordero Alto, where I worked, are located. Sherds scattered on the surface of these sites and the two stratigraphic cuts so far accomplished show that the area was inhabited continuously from the Formative to the Early Nazca period, at which time the population shifted to more spacious, though less easily defended, parts of the valley.

The Juan Pablo style was essentially conservative, remaining, of all regional styles in the Ica Valley, most faithful to its Formative period traditions. It was the most Chavinoid of Early Paracas pottery and at the same time gave special emphasis to non-Chavinoid, locally important motifs such as the fox and vencejo, which had apparently been held over from the Early Ceramic period. It continued to develop its Early Paracas iconography throughout the Middle period, showing little influence of the intrusive Cavernas culture, and well into Late Paracas, during which time it rejoined the main stream of south coast cultural development.

Juan Pablo ceramics form the largest and most comprehensive stylistic group in the Cummings Paracas collection, and offer us an unusual opportunity to witness a gradual evolution of motifs over an extended period of time. To facilitate this study I will divide the Early Paracas period into four phases and limit discussion to the most important motifs of Juan Pablo iconography: the feline, fox, falcon, and vencejo.

THE JUAN PABLO FELINE MASK MOTIF

Double-spout bottles ornamented with a frontal feline mask were characteristic of all Paracas sites in the Ica Valley during the Formative period. They then disappeared from the design vocabulary of Ocucaje and Callango, but at Juan Pablo continued as a major ceramic type throughout the remainder of the Paracas sequence. Our earliest example (146) is transitional in style between the Formative and Early Paracas periods. The mask is rendered in a strongly Chavinoid

146, 147, 148, 149, 150, 151

manner, closely related to that of the late Formative example from Chiquerillo we discussed earlier (97). The features are simplified and less curvilinear, and the fangs no longer go beyond the lip. The red bird-head blind spout, which like the mask motif disappears at Ocucaje and Callango, remains as a characteristic of the Juan Pablo style. It no longer contains a whistle, however, although the vent below the beak remains.

In the second phase (147), the mask becomes more complex and broadened, although it still maintains the button nose and profile ears set well away from the spout. The ears now contain lines that suggest a double meaning of paws, while the more elaborate brow area contains a whisker element above the nose as well as circular pelt markings. Below the wider and more stylized eyes and elongated mouth is a Chavinoid eye pattern flanked by lines indicating whiskers, and at the lower corners next to the outer bands simplified leg and paw motifs may be seen.

In the third phase (148), the trend toward elaboration continues. The brow whisker and the pelt markings become more complex, and the ear-paw elements now crowd the spout. A new ear indication — a curl at the end of the brow — replaces the profile ear, which now seems definitely translatable as the rear feet. The forefeet remain at the corners of the mouth, and the chin area displays more elaborate eye and whisker patterns.

152

From the third phase also comes a rare modeled feline figure (152) that shows the three-dimensional relationship of the elements and makes their arrangement in the mask motif clear. The front legs, for instance, are marked with the same pattern as on the bottles, and the pelt marks extend along the back of the figure behind the head, suggesting the spots in the brow area of the bottle motif. It is interesting to note that a Chavinoid eye pattern has been incised on the breast of the figure at the point where the animal's chest fur would be ruffled, which may explain the placement of the eye patterns below the mouth of the masks.

In the last phase of Early Paracas (149), the trend toward lower, compressed forms is accentuated. The broadened brow area is divided by three whisker elements instead of one, and the area below the mouth is more elaborate and is filled with geometric motifs, which vary widely among examples of this phase. The pelt markings, the ear-paws, and the forefeet usually remain. The blind spout on this bottle is in the form of a human head with a peaked cap. Blind spouts of this type and, more commonly, in the form of red bird or falcon heads are found on all Early Paracas bottles at Juan Pablo. To my knowledge, the human motif appears at Juan Pablo almost exclusively as a modeled head spout during the Early Paracas period. The protruding tongue of the example illustrated may be an early instance of Cavernas influence, not manifested elsewhere in the piece.

In the Middle Paracas period, contemporary with the Cavernas style, Juan Pablo bottle forms lose their gambrel and become further compressed and ovoid (150), showing influence of the Cavernas subglobular type we have already seen in examples from Ocucaje. The three brow whiskers and multiple pelt markings are further elaborated, but all paw elements are absent. The band of geometric motifs that appeared below the mouth in the preceding phase now borders the mask, passing under the handle between the spouts.

[103]

Our Late Paracas example (151) is a low, lenticular bottle having a degenerate feline mask with misplaced canine teeth. It was found in the same grave as a basin-shaped bowl with the distinctive Rio Grande motif of a winged forehead ornament on its sides and a geometric border inside the rim (153).

Though the mask was greatly altered in its long evolution from Formative to Proto-Nazca times, it offers a remarkable example of the persistence of Chavinoid motifs in the upper Ica Valley.

153

THE JUAN PABLO FELINE FIGURE MOTIF

Simplified feline masks confined to the limits of a rectangular panel are a common decorative motif on Juan Pablo bowls. They sometimes have next to them a longer rectangular motif representing a profile feline body. (Motifs of the complete feline do not occur on bottles at Juan Pablo during the Early Paracas period, as they do at Ocucaje and Callango.) Our selected series of examples of the bowl motif shows the same trend toward increased complexity during Early Paracas as we have just seen in the bottle mask. In the Middle and Late periods the motif was subjected to severe simplification and occurs less frequently.

The Phase One example (154) shows a simplified frontal mask with emphasis on the canine teeth. The body has a Chavinoid eye pattern between the legs (resembling the position in the modeled version) and a triangular tail.

The second-phase version (155) shows a considerable advance over the first. Both the mask and body are widened and more elaborate. Two Chavinoid eye patterns now appear below the body, and the tail may be represented by the two elements with curled ends above the back.

Our third-phase example (156) shows a variant in which the body panel is replaced by pelt markings alone, with the tail evidently represented by a conventionalized guilloche, shaped like an hour glass, in the center. The nose has been eliminated and the canine teeth reduced to parallel lines.

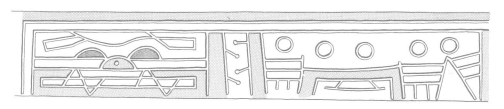

154

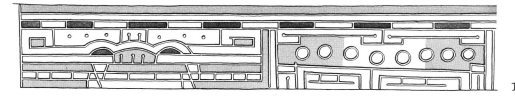

155

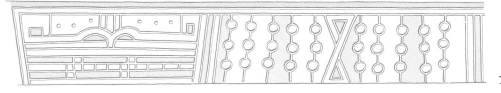

156

157

The final Early Paracas phase is represented by a rendering in which both face and body elements are further attenuated and abstracted (157). The body consists of three eye patterns with tail elements above, but the paws on the legs have been eliminated.

157

The Middle Paracas period is represented by a hemispherical bowl with abstract feline masks (158) set against a background of widely spaced pelt markings. The short, fangless mouth and external whiskers of this version, as well as the vessel's form, betray Cavernas influence.

In the Late Paracas period a radically new stylization of the feline figure, derived from the Rio Grande, was introduced at Juan Pablo: a large-eared, moonfaced cat with looping tail. A rampant pair of these figures may be seen on an unusual, paten-like concave plaque (159), which may have served as a headdress ornament.

158

159

160, 161

THE JUAN PABLO
FOX MOTIF

Although the fox is frequently found on Juan
Pablo bowls, the motif is rarely found on bottles. The
two illustrated are far apart in date — one is from the
first phase of Early Paracas (160) and the other is Late
Paracas (161) — but the basic configuration of the motif is the same. The blind spout is in the form of a long-
snouted fox head, and the figure is incised on the body
of the vessel, spread out like a pelt stretched for drying.
The forelegs surround the head spout, while the hind
legs and the tail hang down to the gambrel. On the
earlier bottle there are Chavinoid eye patterns on each
side of the pelt, giving it the appearance of a frontal
fox mask, in which the tail element becomes the snout.
The body on the Late version is constricted, but in both
cases the modeled head makes identification of the fox
comparatively easy.

Our first example of the fox motif (162) on a Juan
Pablo bowl is transitional in style between the late
Formative and Early Paracas periods. The highly abstract profile figure is divided into head and body
panels similar to the feline motifs. The head (at the
left), however, is in profile, as it was in the Formative
period example from Chiquerillo (100), but without the

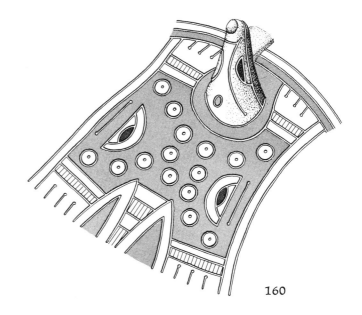

160

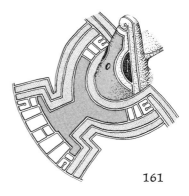

161

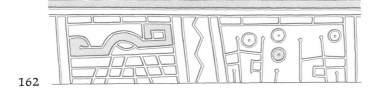

162

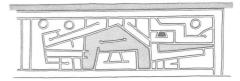

163

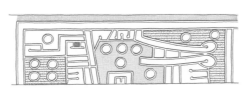

164

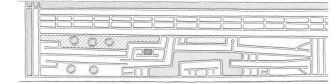

165

166

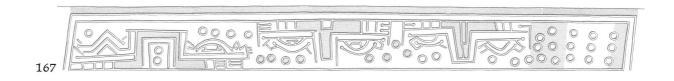

167

foreleg beneath the jaw. The nose, brow, and ear are unified into one element. The body, again like the feline, has both circular pelt markings and eye patterns between the legs — no doubt a deliberate endowment of the fox with feline attributes, as we have seen to be the case with the falcon and serpent motifs.

By the beginning of the second phase of Early Paracas, the fox had undergone considerable transformation (163). The two panels unite to form a single profile figure and the foreleg reappears below the jaw, which now lacks teeth. The eye of the head matches the Chavinoid eye beneath the body, and the foreleg is balanced by a hind leg beneath a triangular tail. Pelt marks are used as space fillers in the background.

A variant of the third phase (164) displays a tendency toward abstraction, though the basic relationship of the feet with the long snout and tail is retained. Pelt marks appear both on the body and in the background. (Incidentally, the diameter of these reed-stamped circles is a pretty good time indicator. They are very large in early Formative, and become progressively smaller throughout the Juan Pablo sequence.)

The fourth phase of Early Paracas (165) is represented by a bowl from the same grave lot as our feline example of this phase (157). The fox is elongated and compressed below a band of teeth motifs. The small pelt-marking circles are restricted to the background above and below the long snout.

In the Middle Paracas period, several new ceramic forms appeared at Juan Pablo. From one of these, a bowl with a loop handle between its widely flaring rim and straight side, I illustrate one of a series of small, degenerate, but traditional fox figures (166), which are set against a pelt-marked background. A more unusual fox motif from the same period (167) is from a deep, hemispherical-based bowl. It is decorated with motifs made up of two half-fox figures, joined back to back and inverted to form a human mask resembling the Cavernas deity face. Again we encounter the Paracas penchant for double meaning.

In the Late Paracas period, the Juan Pablo Early Paracas tradition of stylization finally gave way to new, simpler renderings. One (168), on a straight-sided bowl of the Rio Grande type, is a small abstract figure closely resembling the space-filler animal motifs in Necropolis textiles. Another (169) may be seen on the fox-head-spouted bottle illustrated earlier. Here the animal is shown with both ears in profile, a concept comparable to that on a deep, Rio Grande-type bowl with rattle base from Ocucaje (170). This two-eared stylization is related to the later, Early Nazca treatment of the fox.

168

169

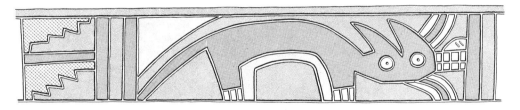

170

171, 172, 173

THE JUAN PABLO FALCON MOTIF

Bottles with a blind spout in the form of a falcon head with feline ears, and with the distinctive falcon markings extending below and behind the eyes, first occur in the Formative period. They become an important and striking ceramic type of the Early Paracas style at Juan Pablo, with the outspread wings, breast, and tail of the bird incised on the body of the vessel below the head. Triangular elements representing the feet are placed at the juncture of the wings and body. Like other Juan Pablo motifs, the falcon evolved from simple to complex, with feline, circular pelt markings on the breast becoming smaller and more numerous. The tail design, beginning with simple panels of Chavinoid eye motifs, grew more elaborate with the addition of elements representing plumage. Our examples represent Phases One (171), Two (172), and Three (173) of the Early Paracas period. The fourth-phase motif became increasingly elaborate and the Cavernas-contemporary version covered the entire top surface of large subglobular vessels; neither is represented in this collection.

174

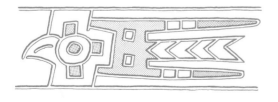

A rare bird motif found on Middle period bowls at Juan Pablo (174) is stylistically related to the Cavernas-influenced renderings of the falcon at Ocucaje, which were based on that center's Early Paracas tradition (105). Similar birds, without eye markings, may be seen on the Late period fox bottle already discussed (161), but a more frequent rendering during the Late period was a greatly simplified bird with a triangular head (175). This example is drawn from the top of a Necropolis-influenced bottle, enriched by a band of geometric motifs and with a fox-head blind spout.

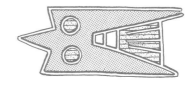

175

THE JUAN PABLO VENCEJO MOTIF

The whippoorwill-like vencejo was, as has already been mentioned, a motif of special importance in the south coast region. It is not found in Chavín art, though it does occur frequently in the Formative period. It continued at Juan Pablo throughout the Paracas sequence and was featured in later Nazca iconography.

Our first example (176) belongs to the last phase of the Formative period. It has a large, double-circle eye and whisker elements curling to meet the beak. The wings, body, and tail are reduced to horizontal geometric components.

An Early Paracas rendering of the first phase (177) follows Formative traditions closely, but the eye is reduced to a dotted circle.

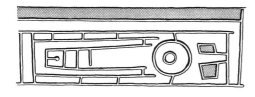

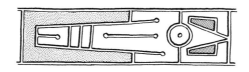

176   177

In the second phase the head was made distinct from the body and the whiskers were drawn as curls on the beak. This example (178) is taken from the same bowl as our fox motif for this phase (163).

By the fourth phase, the strange bird rendering had become more geometri-

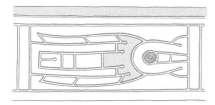

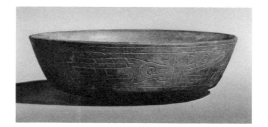

178

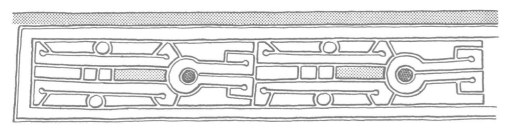

179

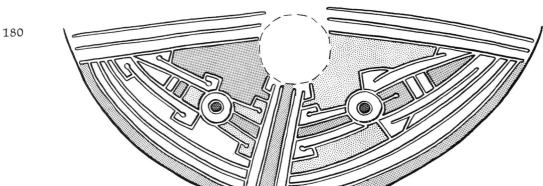

180

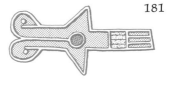

181

cized and elongated. The wing elements in our example (179) are interrupted by small reed-stamped circles.

Two wingless, insect-like versions of this motif (180) are opposed on a Middle Paracas ovoid bottle: they form a design suggesting an abstract, Cavernas-like face where a feline mask is usually placed. The Cavernas stylization of the vencejo encountered at Ocucaje, with two triangular projections for the head (112), is not common at Juan Pablo.

In the Late period, the vencejo, like other motifs we have traced, underwent extreme simplification. The birds now look like clothespins, with the beak sometimes curled back (181) and at other times open (182). They follow the abbreviating trend of Necropolis textile space fillers, but do not resemble the more naturalistic Rio Grande variant sometimes found at Ocucaje, which led directly to the Early Nazca stylization we will see later.

182

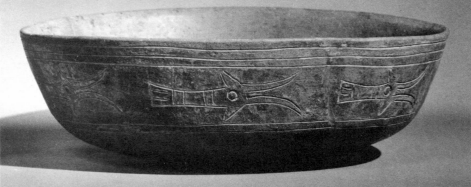

ADDITIONAL NOTES ON THE JUAN PABLO STYLE

Before concluding our brief survey of the Juan Pablo style, I should mention a few additional ceramic types that are characteristic of its Early Paracas period and represent distinctive south coast traditions.

The first, and most controversial, is a dipper-like container (183), which has been incorrectly called a "corn popper" and thought to be of Chavín origin. It does occur in Late Cupisnique, Gallinazo, and Recuay ceramics and continues in Mochica, but it has now been found in the much older, early Formative period of the south coast. It will very likely prove to be a south coast Early Ceramic form, once that period has been isolated and studied, and is but another trait that migrated to the north with the negative-horizon style. Our example belongs to the third phase of Early Paracas. The type disappears by the end of the Middle period.

183   184

Melon-shaped bottles (184) appear to be a Juan Pablo Early Paracas innovation. They occur, together with a wide range of other single-spout bottle forms, with both incised and negative decoration. Our example is from the same third-phase grave lot as the feline effigy bottle, and is ornamented across the top and on the ends with highly abstract motifs. The Maltese-cross-like device on the ends may be interpreted either as a composite of vencejo eye and bill elements, or as feline whiskers. The background and top feature feline pelt marks.

Ceramics decorated with negative spots and bands are characteristic of the Formative period and continued throughout the Early Paracas period at Juan Pablo. The negative spots, like reed-stamped circles, gradually decreased in di-

185

ameter as the style evolved. Negative-decorated double-spout bottles usually have incised and resin-painted blind spouts; negative single-spout bottles have geometric decoration in rings around the neck or in panels on the side. The technique was often used to embellish the sides of bowls below the incised panel or the gap where the pouring lip interrupted the design of Formative bowls (185). Another illustration is an attractive fourth-phase bottle (187) with a vencejo panel on each side. It is interesting to note that by this time the vent in the bird-head blind spout had often been moved to the top of the head, instead of being placed below the beak, where it had served a functional purpose in Formative whistle spouts. The vent was still functional, however, in that it prevented burbling when liquid was poured from the open spout.

We have seen how the ruggedly independent Juan Pablo style strongly resisted acceptance of imported motifs until the final Late Paracas period. When it did adopt new concepts it executed them with finesse — witness the charming, small, human effigy bottle (186) in the almond-eyed, Rio Grande tradition.

186

187

15 THE CALLANGO STYLE

CALLANGO IS located in the southern end of the Ica Valley and, like Ocucaje, some twenty kilometers to the north, is a fairly extensive area including many ancient sites. It was fertile and densely populated in Paracas times, when there was evidently much more water available than there is today. Although there are large collections of Callango ceramics in Peru, comparatively few have so far reached this country. We are fortunate to have a small but representative group of them in the Cummings collection. Though it will not be possible to demonstrate the gradual evolution of style, as it was with the larger Ocucaje and Juan Pablo groups, they are adequate to illustrate the distinctive regional character of ceramics from this part of the valley.

Early Paracas iconography at Callango encompassed all the Formative motifs, including the fox, omitted at Ocucaje during this period, the double-headed serpent, not encountered at Juan Pablo, and the Chavinoid frontal human face, absent at both. At first, the ceramics of the northern and southern areas of the valley were somewhat similar in appearance, but the Callango style soon became much more intricate than Juan Pablo, with a larger portion of the surface of vessels covered with neatly executed incised and resin-painted designs. During the Middle Paracas period some trophy-head-cult motifs appear alongside Early Paracas motifs but, like Juan Pablo, Callango tended to cling to its tradition and reject the Cavernas religion. The few Early and Middle Paracas period ceramics of the Rio Grande de Nazca area that have come to light show a close stylistic relationship to those of Callango, which is logical in view of the geographic proximity of the two regions.

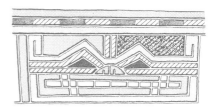

THE CALLANGO FELINE MOTIF

At Callango the treatment of the feline motif on the sides of bowls was similar to that at Juan Pablo, although it differed in detail, tended to be more elaborate, and was rendered in finer, more precise lines (188). The bowl forms were generally wider, with their sides more flaring than on Juan Pablo equivalents.

The most characteristic Callango rendering of the feline often appears on the interior of bowls (189). The body is represented below rather than beside the head, making the figure look seated, instead of standing. The mouth always has fangs, as it does at Juan Pablo, and the body is usually shown with pelt markings

188

[115]

and with rays extending to the gambrel of the bowl. Frequently, as in our example, the triangular forms of the ears, eyes, and brows resemble the Ocucaje stylization. On the sides of the interior of this piece the Chavinoid guilloche also appears, painted without incisions around reed-stamped centers. The exterior bears incised and painted human faces, which we will examine later with other versions of that typical Callango motif.

Another Callango feline figure is incised on a bottle having one spout in the familiar form of an eared falcon head (190). The rendering is similar to, but less detailed than, the one on the bowl. The advanced stylization of the vencejos that appear in the field, the Paul Klee-like handling of the feline, and, especially, the rectangular pelt markings below the jaw suggest that this bottle belongs to the beginning of the Middle Paracas period, reflecting some influence of the Cavernas style. The conservatism of Callango is shown by the fact that falcon-head spouts and vencejo motifs are both found on similar vessels that bear typical Cavernas trophy-head deities with jack-o'lantern faces.

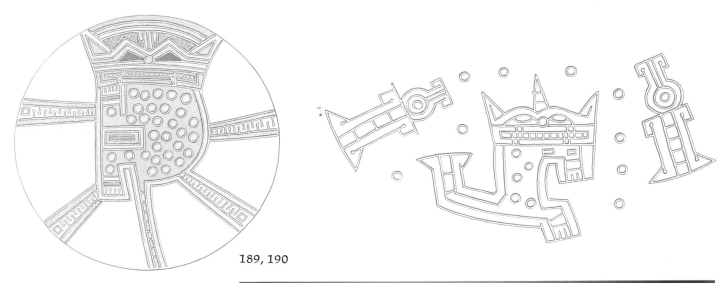

189, 190

THE CALLANGO FALCON MOTIF

Eared falcon bottles, related to those of Juan Pablo but with a different treatment of the wings, body, and tail, were a characteristic Callango ceramic type. On our example (191), the legs extend to the gambrel in front, the wings and body are spread over the dome-shaped top, and the tail appears behind the open spout. Peculiar streamers with hooked sides are painted without incisions between the wings and body. It evidently belongs to a late phase of the Early Paracas period.

A flasklike bottle (192) shows an incised falcon motif in which the head is drawn in profile, and the wings and body are simplified into horizontal and vertical components. The rendering is closely related to contemporary versions in the Rio Grande de Nazca, but can be compared to the Early Paracas Ocucaje motif (105) and the unusual Middle period variant from Juan Pablo (174).

192

191

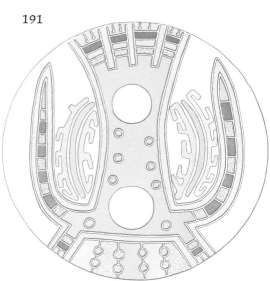

193

THE CALLANGO FOX MOTIF

An interesting representation of the Early Paracas fox motif at Callango is furnished by a large effigy jar featuring two modeled fox heads with incised detail (193). All traces of paint have disappeared, but it appears that the smaller head belonged to a fox figure painted without incisions on the side of the vessel, which itself formed the body of the larger fox. Rather freehand designs are scratched on either side. One is unfamiliar: it consists of concentric squares in the center of a long line with shorter lines branching from it. The other is readily recognizable as a fairly Chavinoid, Early Paracas variant of the vencejo motif.

THE CALLANGO
DOUBLE-HEADED SERPENT MOTIF

194, 195

Double-headed serpents are found at Callango during the Early Paracas period in a stylization similar to that of Ocucaje, though the Callango type was characteristically more complex. Unlike Ocucaje, however, Callango modeled ver-

sions feature an eared-falcon blind spout (194, 195). In both styles the serpent heads show definite feline characteristics such as ears and a snub nose, while the body, in the typical Early Paracas C shape, bears feline pelt markings. The doughnut-like markings appearing along with smaller reed-stamped circles on Figure 195 mark it the earlier and most Chavinoid of the two.

THE CALLANGO HUMAN FACE MOTIF

We saw earlier that the human face motif was important in the Formative period (95). In Early Paracas times it commonly occurs at Juan Pablo as a head

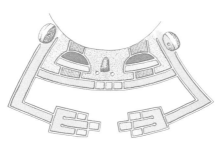

196, 197

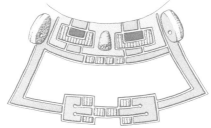

spout, but is absent at Ocucaje. It is, however, a motif frequently found at Callango.

One typical Callango variant appears on single-spout bottles (196, 197). The human head with ears and nose in relief lacks the lower jaw, and has arms with large hands incised on the vessel below the face. The delicacy of the renderings, in contrast to the bold strength and simplicity of Chavinoid versions, indicates that both examples illustrated belong to the Early Paracas time range. The half-round-eyed version is probably the earlier of the two.

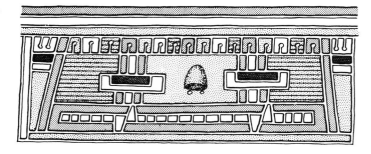

Another characteristic Callango treatment of the human head (198) may be seen on the outside of the bowl with the feline figure on its interior. The faces have rectangular Chavinoid eyes, and a feline-fanged mouth in the tradition of the anthropomorphized Chavín deity (4). Arm and hand elements extend upward alongside the head.

Our last example of Callango ceramics neatly sums up its Early Paracas style and at the same time offers a third version of the human head theme. It is a large bowl decorated with incised and resin-painted designs over its entire interior surface (199). Around the sides are typical Callango feline, human, and falcon heads, and in the center is a strange, invertible human face with Chavinoid eyes both above and below, surrounded by rays and strings of feline pelt markings. Certainly such ornately decorated vessels would have been impractical as food containers. It is, therefore, likely that they were made to serve a special, ritual purpose.

199

16 THE NAZCA CULTURE

200

THE POTTERY of the Early Nazca style, decorated in bright polychrome slip, represented far more than the end result of a technological revolution that had taken place during the Late Paracas and Proto-Nazca periods. The richly varied iconography it bore reflected the parallel development of a dynamic new religion that had revitalized traditional Paracas motifs and added many more of its own. It had succeeded in erasing old regional differences, unifying the populations of the Ica and the valleys of the Rio Grande drainage into one people.

Perhaps as the result of a growing population, which stressed the importance of food supplies, the Rio Grande Paracas people had become increasingly preoccupied with agricultural fertility. They sought to isolate and control through ritual such fundamental fertility factors as the life-giving power of water, the growth potential of seeds, and the productivity of plants. The abundance of all life forms became inseparably associated with fertility, and thus the birds and creatures of the field and water were seen as beneficent spirits toward agriculture.

The Cavernas trophy-head cult had apparently provided a ceremonial means of gathering the life- or soul-force of enemies to be used for the benefit of the collector group. (Among many of the world's peoples, the head, not the heart, has been regarded as the residence of the spirit.) The new Nazca religion expanded this idea and created a pantheon of deities with human, animal, and bird attributes, associated with water, seed, plant, and trophy-head fertility symbols. Prominent among the new motifs were adaptations of the traditional feline, fox, falcon, and vencejo, as well as new additions such as the killer whale, most powerful of sea animals.

Nazca pottery was first confined to the Ica-Rio Grande area but was soon adopted in the Pisco Valley, where Nazca religion was already manifested in late "Necropolis" textiles. It strongly influenced the pottery styles of the Chincha and Cañete valleys and, later, the smaller valleys to the south of the Rio Grande.

The history of the Nazca polychrome ceramic style is almost as long and complex as that of Ocucaje Paracas pottery. Like Mochica, the style was remarkably uniform throughout its cultural area. Unlike their northern contemporaries, however, the Nazca people were at times subject to outside influences that drastically altered their ceramic forms and decoration. The number of Nazca ceramics in the Cummings collection is too small to enable us to trace the gradual evolution of motifs, but will allow us to illustrate the characteristic style of each of the four principal periods.

17 THE EARLY NAZCA STYLE

204

EARLY NAZCA ceramics were simple in form, well made, highly fired, and ornamented with three or more clear slip colors — ranging from almost pure white through cream, buff, tan, orange- and red-browns, Indian red, mauve, gray, and black. The ware was admirably suited to express the fresh vitality of the new style.

At first the prevailing type of decoration was a single conventionalized yet naturalistic motif, repeated against a white or dark background. Such motifs included a delightful variety of vegetables, fruits, birds, animals, reptiles, and fish. The scarlet tanager (200), beans (201), and vencejo (204) illustrated are typical.

Less numerous in early phases, but gaining preponderance as the period progressed, were the more complex fertility deities combining various human, animal, and bird attributes. They were often shown with face whiskers, winged forehead ornaments, and strings of disks hanging beside the head. (Gold equivalents of these attributes, often with a related headdress plume, are sometimes found in graves; apparently they belonged to priests who wore them as part of their ceremonial costume.) The whiskers may be divided into two distinct groups. One, with tufts extended to the side (203), denotes the trophy-head-cult monkey deity, which is often shown in early phases with monkey feet. In the other, the whiskers sweep upward toward the ears (202), a characteristic of the catlike otter (*Lutra felina*). Both types are commonly misinterpreted as feline attributes.

[123]

205

Three early motifs are worthy of special attention since they persisted throughout the entire Nazca stylistic sequence. One is the killer whale, which appears in our example against a white background on a simple double-spout and bridge bottle (205). The drawing expresses more the spirit and movement of this large, rapacious member of the dolphin family than it does its actual compact form. The eye and sharp fangs are emphasized, and the figure has a human arm that, in one of the two versions on this bottle, holds a trophy head. The animal may have personified warrior courage and ferocity to the Nazca, but it is also likely that it represented sea fertility.

Our next motif occurs on a similar bottle with a dark background (206) — a feline figure far more benign than its remote Chavín ancestor: the locally familiar ocelot is represented with the upswept whiskers of the otter. Note that the tongue protrudes as it did in early trophy-head-cult renderings. The combination of feline and otter attributes appears deliberate. Both small animals were to be seen in the fields and near water, and the *pepino* (a variety of cucumber) held in one paw

206

shows the motif's association with agricultural fertility. Representations of this guardian spirit of agriculture became increasingly complex and varied as the Nazca style developed.

Our final and most complex Early Nazca motif is drawn over the top of another double-spout bottle (207). The head has otter whiskers, and its tongue extends to the trophy head held by the hair in the clawlike hands of its outstretched human arms. Other stylized trophy heads are to be seen on its outspread wings and at the base of its bird tail and semihuman legs. The chevron banding on the tail is an identifying trait of the falcon in the Early Nazca style. This strange, bat-like, anthropomorphic otter-falcon demon seems to be drawing out the life-force of the trophy head with its tongue. The motif became a major one in the Late Nazca period, when, as we shall soon see, it was rendered in an even more elaborate form.

207

18 THE MIDDLE NAZCA STYLE

IN THE SHORT Middle period, Nazca motifs, which were always symbolic and seldom had the story-telling quality of Mochica art, became highly abstract. The transformation of style was so fundamental and abrupt that the introduction of foreign influence is evident. The exact source of this influence has not been determined, but the highland Ayacucho area is suspected, since ceramics sharing many Middle Nazca traits have been found there.

208

Few natural motifs, such as birds, survived into this period, and when they did, they were so conventionalized that identification of species is difficult (208). Most Early Nazca deity motifs continued, however, though often in radically different form. Figures that had been strictly animal, such as felines or killer whales, now became anthropomorphic and divided into components that were sometimes rearranged in an abstract manner.

An excellent example, on a small double-spout bottle, is a variant of the agricultural guardian figure, in which the only trait remaining that is possibly feline is a serpentine tail (209). The torso, containing fruit forms, juts horizontally from the neck, and the hips and legs are appended below. A trophy head emerges from the back, sprouting fruit (pepinos) from its mouth — an exceptionally clear example of the life-force fertility concept. The human head has geometric face painting, serpent braids, and a winged forehead ornament in front of its turban-like hat. The hands hold pepper plants, with one fruit placed in the mouth. An insect-like representation of the edible *jiquima* root and its vine appears below the upraised elbow.

An extreme example of Middle period abstraction is found on the sides of a wide bowl (210). A winged warrior deity of the trophy-head cult is represented; its elements, reading from left to right, are: arm and hand holding a bloody war club, sleeve, eyes, brow, headdress with forehead ornament and feline ears, and wing containing trophy heads with pendent darts, one of which forms the tongue (compare this wing treatment to that of the earlier, related otter-falcon on page 125). It will be noted that many figure components present in Early Nazca motifs have been omitted, but to the initiated the symbolism would have remained clear.

From a technical standpoint, Nazca ceramics reached their full development in this period. Their forms were sophisticated, precisely rendered, and beautifully polished. Intricate designs were executed in as many as ten or twelve clear colors, giving a rich, harmonious effect. These high standards of craftsmanship continued throughout most of the Late Nazca period, though fewer colors were generally used. As we shall see, the quality sharply declined in the final, Nazca-Wari period.

209

210

19 THE LATE NAZCA STYLE

211

Modeled ceramics are comparatively rare in all Nazca periods. In the earliest phases they covered the entire range of iconographic motifs, but representations of deities soon became limited to two-dimensional renderings as the concepts grew more elaborate and abstract. By the beginning of the Late Nazca period the range of modeled motifs had narrowed almost exclusively to human subjects. A curious exception in the Cummings collection suggests a mythological theme.

This double-spout bottle (211) has a dome-shaped body slightly modified by pushed-out forms, which are painted to create a multicolored pattern of overlapping pyramid shapes. A small figure of a woman is painted on one side and that of a spotted fox on the other, while between them projects the head of a man, whose arms are painted on the surface of the vessel. The overlapping pattern suggests mountains, and the protruding figure is reminiscent of the Mochica vessel showing Ai-Apec emerging from a mountainside (71). Could this be interpreted as an origin myth? We may never be certain.

The human effigy bottles of the Late Nazca period have a modeled head forming a blind spout and the body suggested by the form of the vessel, with most details painted on. As a group they offer us rare glimpses of Nazca physical types, costume, and occasionally genre. We may rest our interpretive powers briefly while we consider two examples.

One effigy bottle (212) represents an achondroplastic dwarf with jutting

211

212, 213

jaw and flat nose. He has a mustache and beard, and abstract vencejos are painted or tattooed on his cheeks. His apparel consists of a tight-fitting cap and an off-the-shoulder, toga-like mantle in a loud plaid design. He holds a small sash in one hand. You will recall that the Mochica seem to have regarded abnormalities as evidence of the possession of supernatural powers. The same may have applied to the Nazca.

The second example (213) is a more standard one: the face, with its lenticular eyes, mustache, beard, and sideburns, is typical of the Late Nazca style. Long

213

braided tresses spread out over the shoulders and back, and the headdress, bound with a light sash, has two knoblike projections. The man is evidently a warrior, since he holds a throwing stick in one hand and a trophy head in the other. They are painted against a background that may represent a tie-dyed shirt. The formal treatment of back and sides emphasizes the ceremonial significance of the piece, and may or may not reflect actual costume ornamentation. The decoration consists of a broad panel of large deity figures above a checkerboard band, from which hangs a row of trophy heads.

In the Late Nazca period, deities continued to be represented in anthropomorphic form, and the trend of abstraction took a new direction. The heads and bodies of figures were replaced by proliferated motifs, consisting of faces with tentacle-like extensions that curled back on themselves, and pointed elements with diamond-shaped sections on their stems. For the sake of brevity I will refer to these elements as scroll and lancet. Small black symbols, forked like a serpent tongue, were attached to the scroll loops and other parts of the figure, adding to the bristling effect. They represent trophy hair, and by inference the trophy head and its fertility connotations.

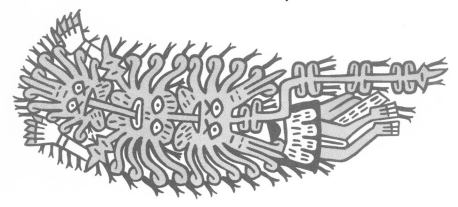

214

It is possible that the new conventions reflected continuing outside influence, but enough transitional motifs exist for me to be inclined to believe that the development was, at least in part, a local one. The proliferated motifs can be most logically explained as an elaboration on traditional Early Nazca deity traits. I refer to the whisker, forehead, and headdress-plume ornaments, which had been becoming increasingly elaborate since their first appearance in Late Paracas times. The plume is usually crowded out of early ceramic renderings of deities. It reappears in Late Nazca in place of the torso, while the other two form the face and head.

To demonstrate this interpretation let us consider the complex deity figure on the back of the warrior effigy bottle (213), which represents a Late Nazca variant of the otter-falcon demon we saw earlier (207). The arms (left) of the flamboyant late version extend forward as they did in the early rendering, but the trophy head is missing, being replaced by trophy-hair symbols attached to the hands and the long, elaborate tongue. The whiskers are more complex, with long lancet elements on the chin where short barbs had appeared earlier, and similar elements extend past the rolled-up eyes. The forehead ornament (compare with Figure 202) has shortened winglike extensions and emphasized scrolls and central face. It extends to the mouth of a very elaborate headdress ornament with long streamer that takes the place of the torso of the figure. The falcon wings of Early Nazca variants are missing, but their trophy-head ornamentation persists in the trophy-hair symbols attached to the scroll and lancet elements. The fleur-de-lis-like motifs extending from the top of the headdress ornament seem to represent sprouting plants. (They are sometimes shown attached to beans in contemporary versions of the feline guardian of agriculture.) Their presence here further emphasizes fertility connotations. Above the legs and rectangular breechcloth of the figure are two feather-shaped elements that may represent a vestige of the falcon tail of the Early Nazca version.

A slightly later, more elaborate version of the same motif appears on a large double-spout bottle with a border of trophy heads wearing fezlike hats (214). In this variant the trophy head has reappeared between the hands, and is now in the form of a complex scroll and lancet face with a sprout symbol emerging from its forehead. Its tongue joins that of the head of the figure, which is a combination of the whisker and forehead elements. An extension of the latter forms the tongue of the headdress ornament, which again features a long streamer and sprout symbols. The two-feathered tail symbol remains the same as in our last version.

Another comparison of Early and Late Nazca conventions applied to the same motif is furnished by the killer whale on a small cup with a band of abstract trophy heads bordering its rim (215). The arrangement of the figure components is similar to that in the first of the two motifs we have just discussed (213). The figure is related to the Early Nazca rendering of the killer whale (205) in its mouth and tail elements. The head is a variation of a frontal killer-whale version (called "bloody mouth" by Peruvianists) that originated in the Middle Nazca period. The tail is a composite of the body fins and tail of the early version, and retains the dark back, central band, and light underside of the animal.

215

20 THE NAZCA-WARI STYLE

216

IN THE FINAL period of the Nazca culture, as in the last Mochica period, ceramic art entered an era of decadence, with only an occasional flare of the technical and creative brilliance that had characterized its earlier pottery. The reason was the same. The south coast was being subjected to an increasing pressure from the highland Tiahuanaco people who were establishing themselves at Wari, not far from Ayacucho. Finally, around A.D. 700, the Wari moved down from the mountains and overwhelmed the Nazca and other coastal cultures.

A tall beaker (216) is typical of the Nazca-Wari style in both its form and decoration. The motif, appearing in two bands on the sides, is a descendant of the Early Nazca feline guardian of agriculture (206). This theme had resisted the tongue-strung, proliferated-head conformity of Late Nazca motifs: the head had remained at right angles to the body, but at the same time the figure had become anthropomorphic and complicated by scroll and lancet elements, including the peculiar sprouting form attached to vegetable and fruit symbols I have mentioned. In the Nazca-Wari period, it too took on the horizontal alignment of fertility-deity motifs.

The arms of the figure are reduced to fringed sleeves and clawlike vestiges of hands that hold sprout symbols. The tongue, mouth, and whiskers are simplified

but recognizable. The face, forehead ornament, and headdress have been resolved into a single U-shaped motif with a fringe of scroll and truncated lancet elements. The three sprout symbols usually attached to the crest of the headdress ornament are represented by spadelike projections. To these are attached two sprout symbols of a different color and a composite motif representing the legs and a sprout-shaped tail.

A motif of the late phase of this period appears on a bottle with widely splayed spouts, a characteristic Wari trait (217). Along with geometric devices, it is decorated with a simple frontal face with pairs of scrolls and lancets on either side. The round eyes and the tongue protruding below the chin are reminiscent of Cavernas deity heads of a thousand years earlier. The motif is difficult to relate to any of the earlier Nazca deities, but may in effect have been a symbol of them all.

217

21 LATE SOUTH COAST PERIODS

FOLLOWING THE decadent Nazca-Wari period, there was a revitalization of the crafts in the South Coast Wari culture. Ceramics displayed a vigorous new iconography and at their best matched the sculptural power of Mochica wares and the polychrome brilliance of the Nazca. Gradually the power of the Wari declined, and after about four centuries its far-flung empire broke up. Local confederations re-emerged on the coast, including the Chimú in the north, the Chancay on the central coast, and the Ica in the south. There followed a period of great city building, accompanied by advances in social organization, engineering, and industry. Craft products, however, tended to be mass-produced and dull by earlier standards. The ceramics of the Ica were competent, but decorated for the most part with the same repetitive geometric motifs as their textiles. Finally, in the fifteenth century, the highland Inca forged a great empire, bringing all of Peru and most of western South America under their sway. An era of renewed prosperity and renaissance in the crafts resulted (218), which was brought to an abrupt close less than one hundred years after it began by the invasion of the Spanish conquistadors. Thus the final curtain was rung down on the long and stirring drama of ancient Peruvian civilization.

218

COLOR KEYS

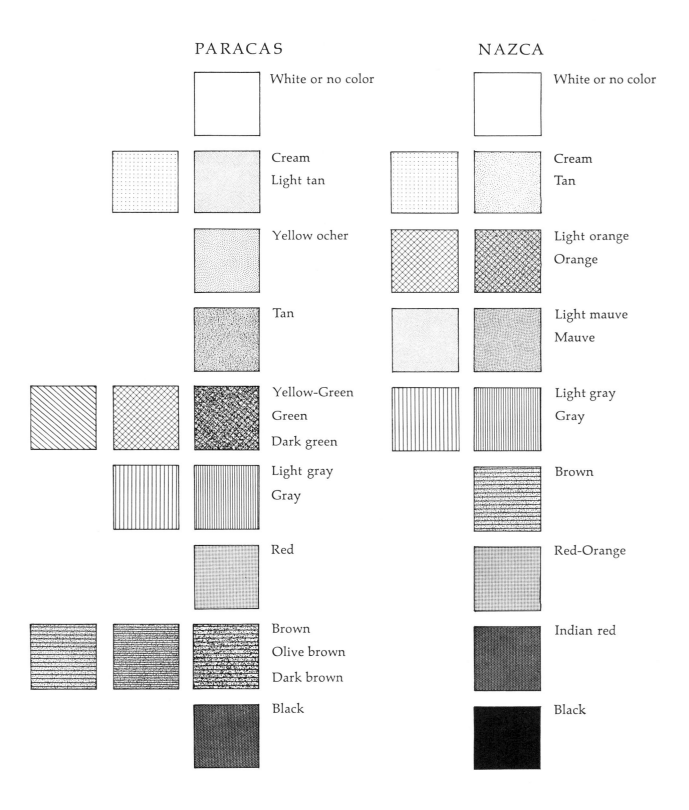

PARACAS

White or no color

Cream
Light tan

Yellow ocher

Tan

Yellow-Green
Green
Dark green

Light gray
Gray

Red

Brown
Olive brown
Dark brown

Black

NAZCA

White or no color

Cream
Tan

Light orange
Orange

Light mauve
Mauve

Light gray
Gray

Brown

Red-Orange

Indian red

Black

NOTES ON THE ILLUSTRATIONS

Objects with accession numbers (e.g. 63.266.4) are in The Metropolitan Museum of Art, given by Nathan Cummings.

1. After Bird, 1962, p. 55, Fig. 4. H. of motif 4½ in.
2. After Bird, 1962, p. 158, Fig. 7. D. of gourd 2⅜ in.
3. After Tello, 1961, p. 204, Fig. 36. H. of motif about 19 in.
4. After Bird, 1962, p. 163, Fig. 12. H. of figure about 19 in.
5. After Carrión Cachot, 1948, p. 136, Pl. XVId. H. of motif about 18 in.
6. After Bushnell, 1957, Pl. 5.
7. After Larco Hoyle, 1945b, p. 12, lower right.
8. After Larco Hoyle, 1945b, p. 13, upper left.
9. After Museum of Modern Art, 1955, Fig. 7. H. 9½ in.
10. After Larco Hoyle, 1944, p. 7, upper left.
11. 63.226.4. H. 7 7/16 in. Cream on orange slip. Probably represents a headdress.
12. After Larco Hoyle, 1944, p. 5, center right.
13. After a photograph (author) of a ceramic from Callango, in the collection of Carlos Soldi, Hacienda Ocucaje, Ica, Peru.

14. After Larco Hoyle, 1945, p. 4, upper left.
15. Detail of Figure 25. The motif probably represents serpent heads (see Sawyer, 1954, p. 27).
16. 64.228.18. H. 5¾ in. Cream and orange slip on orange ware. Depicts a macaw (*Ara macao*).
17. 66.30.2. H. 6 in. Probably from the Santa Valley. White and orange slip on buff ware, with negative decoration. The modeled animal — which might be an armadillo — contains a whistle. The negative designs represent a plumed puma, identified as a sky deity in other contexts, and a bird that, because of the loop on its beak, may be a hawk.
18. Detail of Figure 21. One of four plumed pumas in quadrants.
19. 66.30.3,4. H. 9⅜ and 8⅛ in. Cream on red-brown slip, with negative decoration.
20. 66.30.5. H. 8¼ in. Cream slip on orange ware, with incised lines. A barn owl (*Strix perlata*); note the turned head and lifted foot, giving animation to the figure.

THE NORTH COAST

Unless otherwise noted, all the Mochica pieces are decorated only with two colors of slip—one cream, the other ranging in shade from an orange-red to a dark red-brown.

21. 64.228.7. H. 6¼ in. Decorated with four plumed pumas in quadrants. The drawing is taken from the opposite side.
22. 63.226.9. H. 7½ in. Semireduced brownish ware, with incised lines. The warrior's hands are posed as if he were holding a sling.
23. 64.228.34. H. 7½ in. With fugitive black decoration.
24. 63.226.3. H. 8 in. Represents an anthropomorphic starfish.
25. 64.228.9. H. 8¾ in. With negative decoration. The duck is of the species *Dafila bahamensis*.
26. 64.228.13. H. 8 in. Probably represents a cactus (*Melocactus cactaceas*).
27. 64.228.35. H. 8¼ in. Blackware. Man suffering from acromegaly.
28. 63.226.1. H. 7⅜ in. Unusually opaque slip, with details scratched through the red. Represents crab demons and guanay (*Phalacrocorax bougainvillei*, colloquially called "guano birds").
29. 64.228.14. H. 8⅞ in. Blackware. In the shape of two bowls of food, one filled with crayfish (*Astacus fluviatilus*) and the other with an unidentified vegetable.
30. 63.112.11. H. 12¼ in. The fox warrior, wearing the typical costume of his order, holds a club, throwing stick, darts, and shield.
31. 63.112.8. H. 11 in. The fish demon holds a *tumi*, or chopper-like knife.
32. 63.226.11. H. 9 7/16 in. The headdress ornament is made of two bird skins.
33. 64.228.41. H. 8¾ in. Details in dark brown slip. The man holds a lime bottle and a coca bag. Leaves of the coca bush (*Erythroxylon coca*) were, and still are, chewed with lime for their narcotic effect.

34. 64.228.10. H. 9 in. The form probably represents a turban-like helmet.

35. 64.228.8. H. 8⅝ in. Represents an osprey or fish hawk (*Pandion haliaëtus*).

36. 63.112.6. H. 8⅝ in. Represents an osprey. The drawing is taken from the opposite side.

37. 64.228.25. H. 7 in. With fugitive black decoration. Mochica IV.

38. 64.228.24. H. 10½ in. Mochica III.

39. 64.228.22. H. 12⅝ in. Mochica IV. Nose pierced for ornament.

40. 64.228.21. H. 12¾ in. With fugitive black decoration. Mochica IV.

41. 63.112.9. H. 7 1/16 in. This personage is frequently depicted in Mochica II. Because of his beard, supporters of theories of trans-Pacific migration have suggested he is of Ainu origin.

42. 64.228.30. H. 5½ in. Mochica III. This small moldmade figure of a woman holding a child has no slip decoration.

43. See Figure 60.

44. 64.228.39. H. 8½ in. Mochica III.

45. See Figure 52.

46. See Figure 53.

47. See Figure 56.

48. See Figure 80.

49. See Figure 33.

50. 64.228.36. H. 9 in. Mochica V. The man is chewing coca and holds a coca bag.

51. 64.228.45. H. 10¼ in. Mochica IV. The woman carries her burden by a head strap.

52. 64.228.47. H. 8½ in. Mochica IV. Represents a potter making a jar depicting a prisoner—note the rope around its neck.

53. 63.226.10. H. 8¼ in. With fugitive black decoration and orange slip. Mochica IV. Also in the color plate on page 16.

54. 64.228.43. H. 7½ in. Spout restored. Mochica III. The man carries a dipper-like vessel miscalled a "corn popper" (see page 113) and a rolled mat. His head has deep gouges (a patient recovering from a trepanning operation?).

55. 64.228.44. H. 9 in. Cream slip on orange ware, with fugitive black decoration. Mochica IV. Represents a leper, whose nose and feet are eaten away.

56. 64.228.42. H. 6⅞ in. Mochica V. A hunchback.

57. 64.228.4. From a stirrup-spout vessel. H. 12¼ in.

58. 64.223.192,193. H. of upper clasp 3¼ in. Mochica IV. The animals represented are foxes. One tailpiece has been reconstructed of leather. Note the tailpiece worn by the warrior at the far right of Figure 57.

59. 64.228.33. H. 8¼ in. With fugitive black decoration. Nose restored. Mochica III. Also in the color plate on page 16.

60. 64.228.31. H. 8⅛ in. With fugitive black decoration. Right hand, club top, and piece of shield restored. Mochica III. Also in the color plate on page 16.

61. 63.226.6. H. 12½ in. With fugitive black decoration. Mochica IV.

62. See Figure 30.

63. 64.228.3. H. 11 in. Mochica IV.

64. 64.228.2. H. 10¼ in. Part of one side restored; the drawing shows the opposite side. Metal plates cover the hawk warrior's shirt. A serpent motif (illustrated on page 9) decorates the handle and spout.

65. 63.226.8. H. 9⅛ in. Only cream slip. Right hand, club, crest, and spout restored.

66. 64.228.1. H. 11⅝ in. The drawing restores scuffed areas. Mochica IV. The masks worn by the runners represent, from left to right, a hummingbird, puma, hawk, and fox.

67. 64.228.6. H. 11½ in. Spout restored. Mochica IV.

68. 63.113.4. Detail of a stirrup-spout vessel. H. of whole 9 in. Mochica V. A messenger tying on his headdress.

69. 64.228.40. H. 9⅝ in. Mochica IV. The man holds a lime stick and lime bottle, and has a coca bag slung over his shoulder. The painted cactus, flowers, and serpents indicate a highland setting.

70. 64.228.15. H. 10⅝ in. Mochica IV. A dipperlike vessel miscalled a "corn popper" (see page 113).

71. 64.228.63. H. 8¼ in. Mochica IV. The attendant at the right (head now missing) is an anthropomorphic lizard.

72. 64.228.61. H. 7¾ in. Mochica III. Blackware; the gold inlays set in a black matrix may be modern additions.

73. 63.226.13. H. 8½ in. Mochica IV. Spout and temple restored.

74. 64.228.60. H. 7⅜ in. Mochica IV.

75. 64.228.5. H. 8¾ in. Mochica III. Such raft boats, called *balsas*, made of bound hollow canes, are still used on Lake Titicaca. Note the water bottles behind the figure's foot.

76. 64.228.57. H. 12⅛ in. Some restorations. Mochica V. Yuca, also known as manioc and cassava, is a species of plant, the roots of which are used to make modern tapioca.

77. 64.228.27. H. 10⅛ in. Mochica IV. The nose, lips, and eyelids show punitive mutilation or the ravages of disease. Several varieties of potato are indigenous to the Andean region; this is probably *Solanum tuberosum*.

78. 64.228.19. H. 7¼ in. Blackware. Mochica III. Another version, made in the same mold, has ears added (see Sawyer, 1954, p. 17).

79. 63.226.7. H. 11 in. Mochica IV. Antlers and ears restored. *Cervus nemorivagus*.

80. 64.228.48. H. 9 in. Mochica III. The animal is probably a puma (*Felis concolor*).

81. 63.226.2. H. 9⅜ in. Blackware. The monkeys on the stirrup and the stylized frogs on the shoulder were separately moldmade.

82. 64.228.38. H. 7 in. Blackware.

83. 64.228.53. H. 5¾ in. Black, white, red-brown, and brown slip.

84. 64.228.51. H. 7½ in. Blackware. The figures were individually moldmade and applied. The large figure contains a whistle, with the vent at the juncture of the back and strap handle.

85. 64.228.17. H. 11⅛ in. Blackware.

86. 63.226.12. H. 6⅝ in. Blackware.

87. 64.228.16. H. 7½ in. Blackware.

88. 66.30.7-16. H. of aryballos 4½ in. Terracotta. The grave lot consists of 4 trays (2 with handles), 4 *chicha* jars, 1 aryballos, and 1 footed, loop-handled jar. The aryballos, trays, and 1 *chicha* jar are coated with dark brown slip. The miniature size of these vessels may indicate a child burial.

89. 66.30.6. H. 5⅝ in. Cream, orange, and dark brown slip. Only one side is decorated.

90. 66.30.17. H. 15½ in. White and black slip on buff ware.

91. 64.228.54. H. 6¼ in. Black and red-brown slip on cream. The figure contains a whistle.

THE SOUTH COAST

Paracas colors are all resin-based paints, unless otherwise noted. They are not specified when mentioned in the text, or when the piece is illustrated by a color-keyed drawing.

92. 63.232.6. H. 7¼ in. The identification of the animals is difficult: one has horns, and might be a deer.

93. 62.266.76. 4 1/16 in. Pigment traces not identifiable.

94. 63.232.1. H. 2⅜ in. Yellow ocher and red.

95. 62.266.62. H. 3¾ in.

96. See Figure 4.

97. 62.266.72. H. 7 in. The light tan indicated in the drawing was originally a darker color; traces of black.

98. See Figure 5.

99. Alan R. Sawyer Collection. H. 2⅝ in. Found in the back dirt of a deep huaquero excavation. Brown surface, with traces of red and brownish residue.

100. 63.232.4. H. 3 11/16 in.

101. 62.226.71. H. 6¾ in. Red, cream, and possibly black and brown.

102. 64.228.186. H. 4¾ in. Only red remains.

103. After Bushnell, 1957, Pl. 17.

104. 64.228.90, 91; 93-101; 189; 191. Cerro de la Capilla site.

105. 64.228.97. H. 3¾ in.

106. 64.228.90. H. 3⅜ in.

107. 64.228.189. H. 3⅝ in.

108. 64.228.89. H. 5 in. Cerro de la Capilla site.

109. 64.228.84. H. 4⅜ in. Cerro de la Capilla site.

110. 62.266.68. H. 6⅜ in.

111. 63.232.102. H. 2¼ in. Cerro Max Uhle site.

112. 62.228.188. H. 15⅝ in. Cerro Max Uhle site. Also in the color plate on page 68. The drawings are taken from the opposite side.

113. 63.232.93. H. 5½ in. Cerro de la Cruz site. Also in the color plate on page 68.

114. After Sawyer, 1961, Fig. 4a.

115. 64.228.190. H. 6 in. Cerro Max Uhle site.

116. 63.232.92. H. 1 13/16 in. Cerro Blanco site. Yellow ocher, gray, red, black, tan, and white.

117. 63.232.94. H. 2 9/16 in. Pinilla site.

118. 63.30.21. L. of whole border, including fringe, 110 in.; h. of design unit 9⅜ in. Probably from Necropolis site, Pisco Valley.

119. After a sketch by Wallace in a letter (April 18, 1960) to the author.

120. L 64.69.2. H. 8½ in. Cerro Max Uhle site. The drawing is taken from the opposite side.

121. 63.232.80. H. 6 1/16 in. Cerro Blanco site. The drawing is taken from the opposite side.

122. 63.232.79. H. 2 1/16 in. Cerro Max Uhle site. Interior: cream, 2 shades of yellow, red, green, and black; exterior: cream, red, yellow, and green.

123. From the foot effigy at the far right of the bottom shelf in Figure 129.

124. 63.232.98. H. 3⅛ in. Cerro Max Uhle site.

125. 63.232.97. H. 3½ in. Cerro Blanco site.

126. 63.232.96. H. 3⅛ in. Cerro Blanco site. The two circles at center left are ancient drilled repair holes.

127. The Art Institute of Chicago, Nathan Cummings Collection. H. 2 9/16 in. Cerro Blanco site.

128. 63.232.95. H. 3 1/16 in. Cerro Max Uhle site.

129. 63.232.68-78; L 64.65.91-92. H. of largest bowl 3 5/16 in. Cerro de la Capilla site. Cream, yellow ocher, mustard yellow, dark green, gray, mauve, red, and brown.

130. L 64.65.20. H. 2 3/16 in. Cerro Max Uhle site. Thin red slip under negative decoration.

131. 63.232.61. H. 1¼ in. Cerro Max Uhle site.

132. 63.232.65. H. 2¼ in. Pinilla site. Thin red slip under negative decoration.

133. 63.232.63. H. 2 5/16 in. Cerro de la Cruz site.

134. 62.266.65. H. 3⅛ in. Red slip under negative decoration.

135. 63.232.55. H. 5¼ in. Cerro Max Uhle site. Also in the color plate on page 68.

136. 63.232.56. H. 5⅛ in. Cerro Max Uhle site.

137. 63.232.57. H. 7 5/16 in. Cerro Max Uhle site.

138. 63.232.58. H. 7⅜ in. Cerro Max Uhle site.

139. L 64.65.35. H. 5 in. Pinilla site.

140. 62.266.63. H. 6⅞ in.

141. 62.266.64. H. 5⅝ in. Cerro Blanco site.

142. 63.232.49. H. 7 in. Cerro Blanco site.

143. 63.232.51. H. 2⅝ in. Cerro Blanco site.

144. 63.232.46. H. 6½ in. Pinilla site.

145. 63.232.47. H. 6 in. Cerro Max Uhle site.

146. 62.266.1. H. 5¼ in. Only red remains.

147. 64.228.122. H. 6¼ in. Only red, pink, and cream remain.

148. 64.228.127. H. 6⅛ in. Only red remains.

149. 62.266.9. H. 5 7/16 in. Only red remains.

150. 64.228.178. H. 5¼ in. Red, cream, orange, orange-pink, buff, and black.

151. 64.228.109. H. 4⅝ in. Only red, pink, and white remain.

152. 64.228.119. H. 6¼ in. Only red, pink, and white remain.

153. 64.228.166. H. 2 7/16 in. Only red, pink, and cream remain.

154. 64.228.124. H. 2⅛ in.

155. 62.266.25. H. 2 11/16 in. Negative-decorated interspace. Red-slipped interior.

156. 64.228.104. H. 2⅜ in. Negative-decorated interspace. Red-slipped interior.

157. 62.266.34. H. 2⅛ in. Negative-decorated interspace. Red-slipped and negative-decorated interior. The drawing is taken from the opposite side.

158. 62.266.44. H. 2 7/16 in. Negative-decorated interspace. Red-slipped interior.

159. 64.228.184. D. 4¾ in.

160. 62.266.10. H. 6⅝ in. Partly restored.

161. 62.266.3. H. 6¼ in. Partly restored.

162. 62.266.26. H. 2¼ in.

163. 63.112.21. H. 2 3/16 in. Red-slipped interior.

164. 64.228.106. H. 2 3/16 in. Negative-decorated interspace. Red-slipped interior.

165. 62.266.35. H. 2⅝ in. Negative-decorated interspace. Red-slipped interior.

166. 64.228.113. H. 2½ in.

167. 64.228.165. H. 2¾ in.

168. 64.228.164. H. 3 3/16 in. Only red and pink identifiable.

169. See Figure 161.

170. 63.232.90. H. 3 11/16 in. The drawing is taken from the opposite side.

171. 62.266.6. H. 6⅜ in. Only red remains.

172. 64.228.121. H. 5¼ in. Only red and yellow identifiable.

173. 64.228.126. H. 6¼ in. Only red identifiable.

174. 64.228.163. H. 3 in.

175. 64.228.160. H. 5¼ in. Only red and pink identifiable.

176. 62.266.21. From a hemispherical bowl. H. 2⅞ in. Only red identifiable. Negative-decorated interspace. Red-slipped interior.

177. 66.30.1. From a hemispherical bowl. H. 3¼ in. Negative decoration in interspace and below vencejo panels. Red-slipped interior.

178. See Figure 163.

179. See Figure 185.

180. 64.228.110. H. 4½ in.

181. 62.266.39. From a basin-shaped bowl with a slight gambrel. H. 2⅝ in. Only red and pink indentifiable. Resin-painted dots in interspace.

182. 62.266.37. From a basin-shaped bowl with a gambrel. H. 2⅞ in. Only red identifiable. Red-slipped interior.

183. 64.228.116. D. 7¼ in. Only red and pink identifiable.

184. Lent by Alan R. Sawyer, L 65.78; a pair with 64.228.118 in the Cummings collection, now undergoing restoration. H. 5 9/16 in. Only red identifiable.

185. 64.228.153. H. 1½ in.

186. 64.228.170. H. 4½ in. Only red identifiable.

187. 64.228.158. H. 5⅜ in. Only red and pink identifiable.

188. 63.232.14. H. 3 in.

189. 63.232.13. H. 2¾ in.

190. 63.232.28. H. 5¼ in. No traces of paint.

191. 63.232.27. H. 4 11/16 in.

192. 63.232.10. H. 7 5/16 in.

193. 63.232.43. H. 9⅛ in.

194. 63.232.23. H. 3¾ in. Red, yellow, yellow-brown, brown, and black.

195. 63.232.24. H. 4 5/16 in. Extensively restored. Red, mustard yellow, brown, black-brown, and black.

196. 63.232.8. H. 6 5/16 in.

197. 63.232.10. H. 8⅝ in.

198. See Figure 189.

199. 63.232.22. D. 8 11/16 in.

The colors of the Nazca pieces are slip paints, and are specified here unless the drawing contains all the colors on the object.

200. 64.228.71. D. 7 1/16 in.
201. 66.30.19. H. 4⅜ in. White, tan, brown, Indian red, and black.
202. 63.112.1. H. 7½ in. White, tan, orange, red-orange, Indian red, and black.
203. 64.228.75. H. 4⅝ in. White, cream, tan, mauve, gray, dark brown, brown, Indian red, and black.
204. 66.30.20. H. 4 in. White, mauve, red-orange, and black.
205. 64.228.70. H. 6 11/16 in. The drawing is taken from the opposite side.
206. 64.228.68. H. 6⅞ in. The drawing is taken from the opposite side.
207. 64.228.81. H. 7¼ in.
208. 63.112.2. H. 5¼ in. White, cream, tan, orange, gray, Indian red, and black.
209. 64.228.69. H. 4 9/16 in.
210. 64.228.74. H. 2¾ in.

211. 64.228.67. H. 5¼ in. White, tan, brown, red-orange, and Indian red.
212. 64.228.65. H. 8½ in. Cream, light orange, orange-brown, brown, and black.
213. 64.228.66. H. 9¼ in. White, cream, tan, mauve, gray, orange-brown, brown, red-orange, and black.
214. 64.228.79. H. 6 11/16 in. White, red, and black. The drawing is taken from the opposite side.
215. 64.228.77. H. 2¾ in. White, tan, gray, red-orange, Indian red, and black.
216. 64.228.73. H. 8⅛ in. White, cream, light orange, orange, gray, Indian red, and black.
217. 64.228.78. H. 7 in. White, cream, orange, brown, red-orange, and Indian red.
218. 63.30.18. H. 7½ in. Orange-buff ware with cream, red, and black slip.

All site photographs were taken by the author, except the ones on page 70, which is by Lawrence Dawson, and on page 78, by Pablo Soldi.

The color plate on page 16 illustrates Figures 53, 59, and 60; the one on page 68 illustrates Figures 113, 112, and 135.

SELECTED BIBLIOGRAPHY

The works below will provide the reader with extended coverage of central Andean archaeology. Many have selected bibliographies. In addition to selected general works that should be available in most libraries, a few of the major specialized sources important to the study of north and south coast cultural chronology are listed.

GENERAL REFERENCES

Bennett, W. C. *Ancient Arts of the Andes.* New York, 1954.

Bennett, W. C., and Bird, J. B. *Andean Culture History.* New York, 1949, revised 1960.

Bird, J. B. "Art and Life in Ancient Peru, An Exhibition" in *Curator* II (New York, 1962), pp. 145-209.

Bushnell, G. H. S. *Peru.* New York, 1957.

———. *Ancient Arts of the Americas.* New York, 1965.

Disselhoff, H. D., and Linné, S. *The Art of Ancient America.* New York, 1961.

Doering, H. U. *The Art of Ancient Peru.* New York, 1952.

Kelemen, P. *Medieval American Art.* New York, 1943, revised 1956.

Lehmann, W., and Doering, H. U. *The Art of Old Peru.* New York, 1924.

Mason, J. A. *The Ancient Civilizations of Peru.* Edinburgh, 1957.

Sawyer, A. R. *The Nathan Cummings Collection of Ancient Peruvian Art.* Chicago, 1954.

Schmidt, M. *Kunst und Kultur von Peru.* Berlin, 1929.

Steward, J. H. (editor). *Handbook of South American Indians,* Vol. 2. Washington, 1946.

Wassermann-San Blas, B. J. *Ceramicas del antiguo Peru.* Buenos Aires, 1938.

NORTH COAST
CULTURAL CHRONOLOGY

Ayres, F. D. "Rubbings from Chavín de Huántar, Peru" in *American Antiquity,* XXVII (Salt Lake City, 1961), pp. 238-245.

Bird, J. B. "Preceramic Cultures in Chicama and Virú" in *Memoir 4, Society for American Archaeology* (Menasha, 1948), pp. 21-28.

———. "America's Oldest Farmers" in *Natural History,* LVII (New York, 1948), pp. 296-303, 334, 335.

———. "Pre-ceramic Art from Huaca Prieta, Chicama Valley" in *Nawpa Pacha,* I (Berkeley, 1963), pp. 29-34.

Carrión Cachot, R. "La Cultura Chavín" in *Revista, Museo Nacional de Antropología y Arqueología,* II (Lima, 1948), pp. 99-172.

Collier, D. "Cultural Chronology and Change, as Reflected in the Ceramics of the Virú Valley, Peru" in *Fieldiana: Anthropology, Chicago Natural History Museum,* Vol. 43. Chicago, 1955.

Ford, J. A., and Willey, G. R. "Surface Survey of the Virú Valley, Peru" in *Anthropological Papers, American Museum of Natural History,* Vol. 43, Pt. 1. New York, 1949.

Larco Hoyle, R. *Los Mochicas.* Lima, 1938-1939.

———. *Los Cupisniques.* Lima, 1941.

———. *Cultura Salinar.* Trujillo, 1944.

———. *La Cultura Virú.* Buenos Aires, 1945a.

———. *Los Cupisniques.* Buenos Aires, 1945b.

———. *Cronología arqueológica del norte del Perú.* Buenos Aires, 1948.

Museum of Modern Art. *32 Masterworks of Andean Art.* New York, 1955.

Rowe, J. H. *Chavín Art, An Inquiry into Its Form and Meaning.* New York, 1962.

Strong, W. D., and Evans, C. "Cultural Stratigraphy in the Virú Valley, Northern Peru" in *Columbia Studies in Archaeology and Ethnology,* Vol. 4. New York, 1952.

Tello, J. C. *Chavín, Cultura matriz de la civilization andina.* Lima, 1961.

Willey, G. R. *Prehistoric Settlement Patterns in the Virú Valley, Peru.* Washington, 1953.

SOUTH COAST
CULTURAL CHRONOLOGY

Bird, J. B., and Bellinger, L. *Paracas Fabrics and Nazca Needlework.* Washington, 1954.

Carrión Cachot, R. "La Indumentaria en la antigua cultura de Paracas" in *Wira Kocha,* I (Lima, 1931), pp. 37-86.

———. *Paracas Cultural Elements.* Lima, 1949.

Engel, F. "Early Sites in the Pisco Valley of Peru: Tambo Colorado" in *American Antiquity,* XXIII (Salt Lake City, 1957), pp. 34-45.

Kroeber, A. L. "Paracas Cavernas and Chavín" in *University of California Publications in American Archaeology and Ethnology,* XL (Berkeley, 1953), pp. 318-348.

———. "Towards Definition of the Nazca Style" in *University of California Publications in American Archaeology and Ethnology,* XLIII (Berkeley, 1956).

Menzel, D., Rowe, J. H., and Dawson, L. E. *The Paracas Pottery of Ica.* Berkeley, 1964.

Sawyer, A. R. "Paracas and Nazca Iconography" in *Essays in Pre-Columbian Art and Archaeology* by S. K. Lothrop and others (Cambridge, Mass., 1961), pp. 269-298.

Soldi, P. *Chavín in Ica.* Ica, 1956.

Strong, W. D. "Paracas, Nazca, and Tiahuanacoid Cultural Relationships in South Coastal Peru" in *Memoir 13, Society for American Archaeology.* Salt Lake City, 1957.

Tello, J. C. *Paracas.* Pt. 1. Lima, 1959.

Valcárcel, L. E. "El Gato de agua, Sus Representaciones en Pucara y Nazca" in *Revista, Museo Nacional de Antropología y Arqueología,* I (Lima, 1932).

Wallace, D. T. "Cerrillos, An Early Paracas Site in Ica, Peru" in *American Antiquity* XXVII (Salt Lake City, 1962), pp. 303-314.

Yacovleff, E. "El Vencejo (*Cypselus*) en el arte decorative de Nasca" in *Wira Kocha,* I (Lima, 1931), pp. 25-35.

———. "Las Falconides en el arte y en las ceramicas de los antiguos Peruvanos" in *Revista, Museo Nacional de Antropología y Arqueología,* I (Lima, 1932), pp. 33-111.

INDEX

References to definitions and principal discussions are in *italic* type. Place names appear on the maps on pages 8, 15, and 67; cultural periods are shown on the chronology chart on page 13.